Achieve!

personal effectiveness

in the not-for-profit sector

Mark Butcher

DIRECTORY OF SOCIAL CHANGE

Published by
Directory of Social Change
24 Stephenson Way
London NW1 2DP
Tel. 020 7209 5151; Fax 020 7391 4804
e-mail books@dsc.org.uk
www.dsc.org.uk
from whom further copies and a full publications list are available.

Directory of Social Change is a Registered Charity no. 800517

First published 2003

Reprinted 2004

ISBN 1 903991 23 4

British Library Cataloguing in Publication Data
A catalogue record for this book is available from the British Library

Cover design by Stephen Strong
Text designed by Stephen Strong
Typeset by Stephen Strong
Printed and bound by Antony Rowe Ltd, Chippenham

Other Directory of Social Change departments in London:
Courses and conferences 020 7209 4949
Charity Centre 020 7209 1015
Charityfair 020 7391 4875
Publicity & Web content 020 7391 4900
Policy & Research 020 7391 4880

Directory of Social Change Northern Office:
Federation House, Hope Street, Liverpool L1 9BW
Courses and conferences 0151 708 0117
Research 0151 708 0136

Contents

About the author

Mark Butcher has been a manager, fundraiser and consultant in the not-for-profit sector for eighteen years, during which time he has worked with many national and international agencies. His past customers have included Victim Support, The Guinness Trust, Cyrenians, Citizens' Advice, the European Cultural Foundation and the Probation Service.

He has a specific interest in helping people to fulfil their potential. This has led him to develop a range of training and consultancy programmes focusing on goal setting, positive thinking, communication and influencing skills, time management and creative thinking.

Over the past decade Mark has worked to develop not-for-profit organisations in over a dozen countries including the UK, Netherlands, Belgium, Hungary, Poland, Croatia, Austria, Romania and Bulgaria.

To find out more e-mail markbutcher@blueyonder.co.uk

Acknowledgements

My grateful thanks go out to Bernard Ross who has taught me so much about time management and life, the canon of classical personal effectiveness thinkers such as Alan Lakein and Stephen Covey, on whose wisdom so much good practice is based, my wife Vivienne, who had to put up with me locking myself away to write this book, and not least to the hundreds of staff, volunteers and trustees who have attended my seminars and generously shared their experiences, opinions and strategies on what it takes to live a focused, contented life, filled with achievement.

Foreword

Why this book was written

We live in a pressurised world. There is a broad consensus that our society is more work oriented than ever before – that people work longer hours, that they are more stressed, that our culture promotes overwork and over commitment. It is true of society at large, and it is increasingly true of the not-for-profit sector. More targets, more emphasis on outcomes, greater competition for funding, increasing requirements to monitor and evaluate – these factors, together with a powerful trend towards greater professionalism and tighter regulation of the sector, have all increased the pressure on trustees, managers and front-line staff. There is pressure to perform, to be effective, to achieve. In short, the not-for-profit sector is a much more challenging place to work in than it was ten or fifteen years ago.

The results of this pressure can be damaging indeed. Some academic studies suggest that a decline in performance of anything up to 25% will result for those very busy people who repeatedly work late, regularly spend long hours travelling and who often take work home at the weekend. Think about the implications: if you fit this profile, then your job is being attempted by someone who is only about three-quarters as intelligent, sharp, focused and capable as you. And that someone is, of course, you! We need strategies to cope with this increased pressure, or the results for individual workers are likely to include more mistakes, increased stress-related illness, even, ultimately, burn-out. From the point of view of employing organisations, failure to equip personnel with the tools they need to remain effective in an increasingly demanding world will mean a struggle to achieve goals and difficulties in fulfilling the mission. This book was written specifically to offer a programme and toolkit to help.

Who is this book for?

Over the past ten years I've talked to hundreds of people working for charities, community groups, local authorities, partnerships and voluntary agencies about the factors which impact on their ability to give of their best. Managers, trustees, front-line workers, volunteers – all face similar challenges, such as leaving work with the to-do list unfinished, spending the day firefighting crisis after crisis, racing to hit deadlines, drowning in paper or struggling to satisfy everyone who demands attention. The result is all too often a feeling of being overwhelmed and stressed to the point where mistakes can be made and life stops being fun.

If you suffer from any of the symptoms listed above, then there will be something in this book for you.

The benefits

This book is designed to give you the tools and strategies to ensure that

➤ your own performance improves;

➤ team results improve as you share the techniques with colleagues;

➤ you will be equipped to deal with increasing work pressure and still have more time for yourself and your loved ones;

➤ you will develop practical strategies to overcome challenges;

➤ you will gain more personal control over your day, and your life, and experience less stress;

➤ you will gain clarity about what you want to achieve, set realistic and attainable goals and create a personal vision based on your values and roles;

➤ you will learn how to balance long-term and short-term priorities;

➤ and you will be shown how to survive the heat in the kitchen!

This book includes sections on how to organise your day, limit interruptions, achieve more from meetings, eliminate procrastination, handle the torrent of faxed, e-mailed, and written material which passes over your desk and a host of other specific and practical strategies.

This book will examine your behaviours

Effective and successful people behave in clearly identifiable ways. As they go through life they apply the principles of achievement. Each of the first eight chapters of this book deal specifically with one of these principles. The principles are designed to help us deal with overly demanding colleagues, chaotic workplaces, crammed schedules, mounting stress and the many other situations, circumstances and issues which prevent us from operating at our best. More fundamentally they address specific behaviours, the application of which help us decide what we want from life and create a programme to achieve it.

How to get the most out of this book

Approach it with an open mind

Some of the thinking in this book is based on the golden principles of time management that have been around for much of the last quarter of a century. They've lasted that long because they work, and because they are based on common sense. Some of the thinking, however, is new. You may not have encountered it before, and you will need to approach it with an open mind if it is to benefit you.

Make a commitment to change

Each chapter addresses a different aspect of behaviour. Behaviours – the way we think and act as we go through life – underpin how much, or how little, we achieve. There is an old saying, 'If you always do what you've always done…you'll always get what you've always got'. This book will repeatedly ask you to change your behaviours, to try new things and new ways of thinking. Change, particularly behavioural change, is hard. If you are not committed to give the techniques in this book a chance and stick with them while you bed them in, then don't waste your time reading the book! If however you genuinely want to achieve more with less pressure, accept that the price of this progress is commitment to change.

Read each chapter twice

Read it once quickly to get an overview. Then go back and read it again. Complete the exercises. Think carefully about the issues. Identify how you can apply the lessons to your own situation at work and at home.

Ruin the book

This book is not designed to be kept as a pristine work of reference. It is designed to be used as a tool to change your life! So read it with a highlighter or red pen readily to hand. Scribble on it, mark it up, underline key paragraphs or sentences. Interact with this book to get the most benefit.

Keep the book

It's not designed to be kept pristine, but it is designed to be kept. The greater the impact the exercises in this book have on your attitude, thinking and behaviours, the more you'll want to change. But the greater the change, the harder it is to maintain. So go back to the book, repeatedly, to remind yourself of the commitments you've made. Put aside some time every month to review your progress against the changes you have decided to make and the techniques you have decided to implement.

At the very end of the book I've included a guide for you to create your personal effectiveness master plan. This is optional. It may be that you feel you've made enough notes, scribbles and lists in the body of the book itself to do the job. That's fine. Personally I like to pull everything together, once the thinking has been done, into a single strategy. Not only does this help to reinforce the key messages I've taken on board and commitments I've made, but it also makes reviewing and modifying my plans easier. Choose which system works best for you.

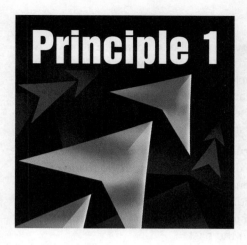

Principle 1

Clarify ...

... what you want from life and work

Overview

In this chapter you will:

➤ discover why the ladder of success is only meaningful if it is leaning against the right wall

➤ consider the universal truth that the direction your life is heading in is probably more important than the speed at which you are travelling

➤ identify the three pillars of personal vision

➤ think about your dearest values

➤ develop a clear and prioritised set of personal goals that reflect these.

Where are you heading?

'Would you tell me, please, which way I ought to go from here'
'That depends a good deal on where you want to get to,' said the Cat.
'I don't much care where ~' said Alice
'Then it doesn't matter which way you go' said the Cat.
' ~ so long as I get somewhere,' Alice added as an explanation.
'Oh you're sure to do that,' said the Cat, 'if you only walk long enough'.

Alice's Adventures in Wonderland, Lewis Carroll

Just like Alice, we too are on a journey. It's called life. And just like Alice, if we are to arrive successfully, we need to be clear about our destination and our direction. If we're planning a driving holiday do we randomly point the car and just drive until we're out of petrol? Surely before we start we need to be clear whether we're heading for Cornwall or Carlisle, as this will determine whether we turn left or right at the bottom of the road. Our destination will govern our *route*. In the same way, the kind of achievement we want in our life will determine the actions we take. Unless we have clarity about what we want to achieve, we can't take control, and we run the risk of drifting along. If we are to take charge, and build a programme which helps us achieve more of the things we want, we need to ask certain questions and get clear answers. What do we want? Where are we going? When do we want to get there? As Mark Twain said, 'If you don't know where you are going, you are almost certain to end up somewhere else'.

And here is something of a moment of truth. We are of course already on our life journey. And where we are *now* depends on the decisions that we made (or didn't make) *yesterday*. Or last year, or ten years ago. The job we do, the partner we are with, whether or not we have children, the places we've seen, the experiences we've had, the debt we're in (or not), all depend on the roads we have chosen, the decisions we've taken in the past.

So of course it follows that what we have in our lives *tomorrow*, and what kind of life we have in the future, will depend on the decisions we make *today*. Have you made any life-changing decisions today? Or yesterday? In fact, when did you last sit down, take stock, decide what you want and fix on an achievable plan to get it? Maybe it's time to decide where your next destination will be and take *control*. Don't be a passenger on this journey. The car is yours. Isn't it time you took the wheel?

Creating a personal vision

Life isn't about finding yourself. Life is about creating yourself.

George Bernard Shaw

It is of course impossible to tell exactly what the future holds for us. Perhaps the only way to come close is to do everything you can to create your own future. Many of us are used to thinking of business planning as an appropriate activity at an organisational level. I'd like to argue that it can work at a personal level too. And as with any business plan, we need a clear *vision* if we are to put a programme of activity in place to achieve our personal plan. If you are not clear about the kind of life you want, it will be very hard to make it happen. As Socrates said, 'the unexamined life is not worth living'. Creating (and achieving) a life-enhancing personal vision for the future demands clarity on three counts:

1 The roles you play in life

This helps to clarify your responsibilities, the network of ties that bind you, and the people who depend on you and on whom you depend. Whatever you choose to do with the rest of your life, it will impact on others. It's good to know the consequences for them and for yourself before you start.

2 **The values that govern how you want to live your life**

Do you want to earn a large salary, and enjoy the material trappings that this would bring, or are you motivated by the chance to improve the lives of those less fortunate? Is your career or your family the most important thing in your life? Are you driven by spiritual, emotional, physical or intellectual needs? Your answers will fundamentally affect the shape of your plan. Think of these questions as the map and the compass which help you to plan your journey. Your roles and values set the broad direction of our travel.

3 **Your goals**

Think of these as the ultimate destination and milestones along the way. Your goals are the achievements, the outcomes which will bring personal satisfaction, fulfilment and happiness.

Step 1: map your roles

All the world's a stage,
And all the men and women merely players:
They have their exits and their entrances;
And one man in his time plays many parts.

William Shakespeare

In some ways the various roles we play represent the sum total of our being. We take on and put aside roles to suit specific circumstances and situations; parent, manager, sibling, friend, adviser – each demands a different kind of behaviour, different levels of responsibility, different kinds of accountability, and sometimes quite conflicting thought patterns, feelings and responses.

If we are to plan an appropriate future we need to know who we are, and understand where exactly we sit in the complex web of relationships that surrounds us.

I'd like you to consider the roles you play:

➤ Those that are currently at the forefront – these are your key responsibilities and relationships.

➤ Those that you'd like to spend more time on but currently don't – for example, perhaps there is a role as son or daughter that hasn't had all of the attention that it deserves in recent times.

➤ Those you're comfortable with, or even live for – this category could include parent, passionate environmentalist, local councillor, churchgoer, football fan, or aficionado of music, art or cinema.

➤ And those that you're not happy with – perhaps some change is required; either in the form of modifying the role, or leaving it behind altogether. Do you need to move on from a job or a relationship?

And what about those roles that you'd love to play, but currently don't, such as writer, student, traveller, teacher, actor, artist, adventurer?

Some of the most common roles that people identify for themselves are:

Parent	Partner	Son/Daughter
Husband	Wife	Other family member
Friend	Professional	Trustee
Homemaker	Breadwinner	Adviser

Mark Butcher's Roles:

Father, husband, son, uncle, sibling, consultant, fundraiser, trainer, musician, company director, graphic designer, coach, friend, writer

Make your own list in the space below.

My main roles are:

When you've listed your roles, I'd like you to try and prioritise them. Simply place a '1' in the box to the right of your most important role, the one which would cause you the greatest pain to give up. Put a '2' in the box to the right of the next most important and so on. We'll come back to this analysis a little later in the process.

Step 2: confirm your values

Our lives begin to end the day we become silent about things that matter.

Martin Luther King Jr

The key to what you really want

An understanding of your prime values is important if you are to work out what you *really* want from life. Unless you are basing your life programme on your real values, dissatisfaction, unease and unhappiness all may result. It's no good working as a freelancer if you need job security. It's no good finding job security if you crave risk. And it's no good building a career in the City if you want to raise pigs in the country. We need to make our values explicit, to identify and confirm what is important to us, and to use this thinking to create a platform on which to build our future.

Value bases

There are probably three main value clusters on which to base your future. I have called these broad categories career, cause and quality. We draw down values from each of these areas to form a personal value base.

Career

If your current value focus lies in this area, you will be ambitious; you will want to reach the top of your profession; you may want to make a lot of money; you'll certainly want to be seen as successful by others; and you'll tend to talk about and think about work a lot of the time.

> **Case study:** Fiona is a typical career person. She works long hours as the chief executive of a regional charity for older people. Evening meetings are common and work taken home for the weekend the norm. 'I suppose work does drive me' says Fiona. 'My partner is involved in a similar organisation and we always seem to end up talking shop over dinner. We'd both like a family one day, but that day always seems to be tomorrow'.

Cause

Not all values are about career. In fact, on your deathbed, the only words I can guarantee you won't say will be 'I wish I'd spent more time at the office'.

For cause-driven people, making a contribution to the lives of others is the key motivator. Teachers, doctors, church ministers, nurses, campaigners, lobbyists all tend to be driven to a degree by their cause. If you care deeply about the environment, child poverty or the welfare of older people; if you advocate for the cause in conversation if you try to persuade others why they too should care, then it may be that spiritual or social cause-driven values are those closest to your heart.

> **Case study:** Beverly left university with an excellent degree in engineering. An IT specialist, she was headhunted by a number of blue chip companies both in the UK and the US. However, she turned them all down, despite the fabulous salaries on offer. 'Making money was never really what I cared about. I wanted to find some work that would make a difference somehow.' Now Beverly works developing computer and Internet networks with poor communities in the third world.

Quality

Those driven by quality-focused values care about the quality of their lives. If your work has been chosen because you enjoy it, but you don't let it dominate your life, if you try to balance family life, career demands and you still find time for a social life, then you may be a quality-driven person.

> **Case study:** Three years ago Kevin was teaching music full time at a further education college in the north west of England. One day he decided that he'd had enough, and immediately began to look for ways to build a more holistic life, less focused on work. 'A part-time post came up, and I took it. It meant less money, but the freedom to do other things with my time more than outweighs the fact that I've now got a smaller car and we'll holiday in Skegness this year instead of going abroad.'

Three things to consider:

> ➤ None of the categories, or the values within them are 'better' than the others. This book is not about ethical choices. It is about personal choice. Your values reflect who you are and therefore some values will mean a lot to you, whereas others will not.

> ➤ Your *value mix* will be a complex and personal one, drawn from all three value categories. You are likely, however, to demonstrate a bias towards one of the categories at any specific time. An opportunity lies in being able to identify your priority category and focus there.

> ➤ As we move through life's phases, we move in and out of the value categories. As we learn, grow and change, as experience and circumstance impact on us, our values tend to change. Where you are now represents a snapshot on a journey.

It is important that we consider and then confirm our values as this will guide us in step 3, when we begin to make concrete plans. It is important that those plans reflect, and are true to, our real values. If this is not the case, then any achievements we make will mean little. The fruit of our endeavours will taste bitter, or have no taste at all.

Mapping your values

In the following exercise we have identified some common motivating values, expressions of the sometimes unstated beliefs that underpin one's approach to life. First review my list. Then, tick those values that you think would form the foundation of a fulfilling and satisfying life for *you*. You can add other value statements if we haven't covered all those that you think are important. Then try and weight the values that you have selected by giving each a score out of 10. Base this not on whether the chosen values currently loom large in your life, or on what others might think or expect, but on how you feel, deep down, you'd like to live your life. There are no right or wrong answers here – it's a personal choice.

A good life would be one which was based on:

	Importance to me in terms of how I would like to live my life (out of 10)
Financial security and/or greater wealth	☐
Intellectual challenge and/or personal development	☐
Family life	☐
Having a close and loving relationship with a special person	☐
Having a vibrant social life with many friends	☐
Self expression and creativity	☐
Taking good physical care of myself	☐
Taking care of others close to me	☐
Contributing to my community	☐
Success in my chosen career	☐

Your results should serve to give you a rough template on which your values are made explicit.

How are you living?

The next stage is to monitor whether you are living life broadly according to your values, or whether you've wandered off track. In the next table we've added an extra column. In this column give yourself points out of 10 to determine *how you are living* (with 10 representing complete adherence to a particular value and 0 indicating that the value plays no part in your current lifestyle). These scores should represent the reality of your life. You will need to be scrupulously honest with yourself. Before scoring, you might like to think about the values in the following terms.

Financial security

If you regularly spend less than you earn, you have no credit card or hire purchase debt, you have made adequate pension provision and you've got savings to cover any big expenditure items on the horizon, then award yourself 10 out of 10. If you've got an overdraft and some other debt, but it's under control, you have a programme to get back into the black and you're sticking to it, give yourself a relatively high mark, say 6 or 7, because although things may not be perfect, you've got your finances largely under control. If your debts are spiralling out of control, score yourself at the low end of the scale.

Intellectual challenge

Ask yourself whether you get enough intellectual stimuli, either from your job or your hobbies. Have you always wanted to do that degree, but tended to put it off for one reason or another? Do you find enough time to read, to think and talk about the issues of the day? If you get enough intellectual challenge to satisfy, then score highly. If you'd like more, then pick a number in the middle of the range. If you feel that you have been clinically brain dead for as long as you can remember and are desperate for more stimulus or challenge, score a low mark.

Family life

Do you feel that you see enough of your family? Do you ever feel guilty because you don't phone parents or siblings enough? Would you like to feel closer to members of your family? How is your relationship with your own children? Do you spend enough time with them? Is it quality time or are you too tired to play at the end of a hard day? Are you putting off having children to further your career, and how do you feel about this? Once again, if you feel that everything is good in this area, score highly; if you feel you would like to change your behaviour for the better, score at the other end of the scale.

Having a close and loving relationship with a special person

Relationships need to be nurtured and fed, or sometimes they wither and die. This book is not about relationship counselling by any means, but it seems common sense that if you always treat your partner the way that you did when you first met, and vice versa, the relationship will retain a lot of its spontaneity, thrill and joy. But we often neglect relationships in order to deal with more urgent issues. What's more important, finishing that report or surprising him/her with a special meal for two? Score as before – I'm sure that you've got the hang of the process by now.

Having a vibrant social life with many friends

All work and no play make Jack and Jill so dull! Do you get out enough? Is your social life varied enough? Are you able to keep in touch with old friends?

Self expression and creativity

Have you always wanted to write the next great European novel; or would you just like more space to make Lego models with the children, join an amateur dramatics group or spend more time in the garden?

Taking good physical care of yourself

The stress of the hurly burly sometimes means that we forget to look after ourselves as well as we might. Eating, drinking and exercise habits – how are you doing in these areas? I'm not suggesting that you should aspire towards some Olympian ideal of physical perfection. Simply consider how fit and healthy you are for your age, and whether you could make any improvements. Would you like to do more – sign up for a pilates class, join a gym, cut back on the red wine? Even small changes can make a difference.

Taking care of others close to you

Do you have family, friends or colleagues who depend on you? Are you driven to help others? Do you do enough, or do you want to do more?

Contributing to the community

Is it time to put something back? Do you want to volunteer your time or skills or donate to a cause?

Success in your chosen career

Are you on track? Or do you feel a bit stuck in your present job? Do you need a complete change of direction? Or just a way of reinvigorating your current career track, such as training?

Now that you've had a chance to think about some of these issues, score yourself in the right-hand column below. When you've finished, compare this 'performance' score with the 'importance' score you made earlier.

	Importance to me (out of 10)	How am I living? (out of 10)
Financial security and/or greater wealth		
Intellectual challenge and/or personal development		
Family life		
Having a close and loving relationship with a special person		
Having a vibrant social life with many friends		
Self expression and creativity		
Taking good physical care of myself		
Taking care of others close to me		
Contributing to my community		
Success in my chosen career		

What does this tell you?

Now consider the results of the exercise. If any of the value statements show a great disparity between your 'importance' score on the left and your 'performance' score on the right, there might be a message for you. Are there things that need to be put right, decisions to be made or behaviour changes to ask of yourself or others? If the 'importance' score is significantly *higher* than the 'performance' score, it may be telling you to change your behaviour in order to allow scope for a value that is important to you. If the 'importance' score is significantly *lower* than the 'performance' score, it might suggest that you should do less of something or *stop* doing it altogether, as you are spending too much time on something which is not important to you.

This exercise works alongside the thinking you did about your roles in that it helps you to create a platform on which to shape a better future. It will suggest areas in which you may want to focus when you consider your future *goals*.

Case study: Kay, a manager within the social services directorate of a county council, completed the exercise and found the results illuminating.

'I'm a single parent, so the issue of financial security is very important to me. I gave it an 8 score in terms of its importance, but only managed 3 when I considered how I was doing. Clearly some remedial action was needed concerning my credit card usage! For family life I scored 10 for importance but only 7 in terms of how I act. I don't visit or call my brothers and sisters half as much as I should. It seems that they are always running after me! The value is important to me, but I definitely feel my lifestyle doesn't reflect this – which leads to guilt!

I scored 'close relationship with a special person' as 0 in the 'performance' column – which normally would be pretty worrying! However, having recently got out of a long-term relationship, I don't feel ready for another one. Right now, finding a special person definitely scores a 0 in terms of importance.

Perhaps what I found most interesting was that I ranked one of the values relatively *low* in terms of overall importance – but I was living my life as if it was *high*. This was 'success in my chosen career'. It was my intention to apply for a promotion which has come up. I could certainly do with the money, and I stand a great chance of getting the post. My performance score for this value is high, because I'm planning my life around it pretty much. But my children need me around right now. The new job would mean more travel and more time away from the boys. I've come to the conclusion that career progress is relatively unimportant and will have to wait for a couple of years until we're all back on our feet emotionally. Comparing 'importance' and 'performance' scores for my career has helped me realise that I need a different plan. I've decided not to go for the new job. Maybe we'll have less money for a while, but we'll be with each other more'.

Values statement

Consider the thinking about your values that you've just done. In the space below, try and summarise and crystallise your value base by coming up with a personal statement of values. You may like to think in terms of the three value categories we talked about earlier (career/cause/quality) and how they relate to you. Or react to the 'importance/performance' analysis that you've just completed. Write a paragraph which makes clear your personal set of values and beliefs and how these will impact on your future life.

My key values are:

_____

_____

_____

_____

_____

Step 3: set goals

In my experience the goal factor is the most important distinguishing characteristic of truly effective people.

Executive Coach, Jenny Ditzler

In the long run, men only hit what they aim at.

Henry David Thoreau

What are goals?

Goals are your expectations, needs and desires made manifest. They are the specific outcomes and results that, if achieved, will make a significant difference to the quality of your life. A goal may be a new relationship, a better job, a new experience or a completed project.

The late Cardinal Basil Hume used to say that there were only three types of people in the world:

➤ Those who were brilliant. They would almost certainly be successful in life.

➤ Those who could spot problems or solve them. They would succeed, but only if they worked very hard.

➤ And those he admired most of all, who were not necessarily brilliant or able to spot a problem or solve it, but who made up their minds to achieve a single objective. They never failed to succeed.

Goals are not wishes or vague intentions. A goal is something that you can influence, it is concrete and you can make it happen by taking action. To bring fulfilment and satisfaction at the highest level, goals should be linked to your most important roles and reflect your key values. Goals that spring from your most dearly held values are usually those that generate the most excitement, passion and commitment. And if you bring those qualities to the task you'll be astonished at what you can achieve.

How to set goals

How many times have you set yourself a New Year's resolution, only to find that you've failed by the end of January? It's happened to all of us. Does this happen because we're not committed enough? Probably not, especially as we tend to choose as New Year's resolutions those things that would really make a difference if only we could stick to them. So if it is not our initial motivation which is at fault, what's going wrong? The reality is that modern life is busy, stressful and challenging. It is filled with people and situations that demand our attention. Put simply, it gets in the way of taking the action that would make a real difference.

In fact goals are vulnerable and fragile things. If left to the pressures of twenty-first century life they are unlikely to survive long without help. They need protecting. There are eight stages to setting and achieving goals successfully. I call it ...

The eight-stage goal survival plan

1 Goals should be contextualised

It's easy to get drawn into life pursuits which do not necessarily serve our deepest inner needs. Are you working to live or living to work? Have the expectations of others superceded your own vision of how life could be? Have you taken a wrong turning? Or do you feel that you are on track, in a career that is compatible with your strengths and gifts, and that your use of time allows you to fulfil your most important roles as well as you can?

Case study: Karen was the head of corporate fundraising for a major national medical charity. She had worked hard to reach her position, loved her work and prided herself on the results she gained, the professionalism of her approach and the expertise she had developed. Most of her goals were career focused. Her most important goal was to hit her fundraising target of £1,000,000 for her employers. Her most important relationship was with Michael, her son, who was severely dyslexic. She had heard of a revolutionary new approach to the treatment of dyslexia which could bring tremendous benefits to Michael, but it would mean moving to America for up to a year. Her commitment to her work, the challenge of selling the house, which the family loved and in which they were very settled, the cost of paying for the treatment, all contributed to what she later described as her 'dithering'. Karen went through the process we've described above and at its completion was in no doubt that the only appropriate thing to do was to sell the house, quit her job and move to the US for however long it took. There would always be other jobs, always other houses. There was only one Michael.

2 Goals should be recorded

You need to write them down for a number of reasons. At the most basic level, you'll forget them if you don't. More importantly perhaps, writing them down serves to make them real. Capturing your goals in this way can be seen as a sort of contract with yourself, a confirmation of your commitment to do what is necessary to achieve the goal.

In a well-known study, graduates from Yale University were questioned about their future plans. Only 4% had written down their goals. Twenty years later, the group was revisited and the researchers discovered that this small group appeared to be happier and more content than the 96% of their classmates who had not bothered to record their key goals in life. Furthermore, it became clear that the goal-oriented 4% had achieved more wealth than the unfocused 96%, although they were not necessarily brighter or harder working.

Many writers on personal performance claim that the 4%, and people like them, have an ability to 'attract' what they need to realise their goals. I don't believe that this is strictly the case. Rather, I think that the world is filled with opportunity. Almost every day presents opportunities to build relationships, learn something new, take a risk, or make a crucial decision. But because these chances rush by we miss them. Someone who has thought clearly about their goals and written them down is better placed to notice these opportunities and grab them.

3 Goals must be SMART

In other words, goals need to be **S**pecific, **M**easurable, **A**chievable, **R**elevant, and **T**ime based.

Specific

If your goals are vague or hard to measure, then it might be difficult to decide whether you are on track. And that in turn can lead to demotivation and a half-hearted approach.

Non-specific goals	Specific goals
Spend more time with the children	Do the bedtime story 3 times a week
Get fit for the summer	Run for 1 mile within 10 minutes
Reduce my debt	Pay off £1,000 from my credit cards and reduce the amount I spend on clothes by 50%

There are clear *disadvantages* in expressing goals in the non-specific way shown in the left-hand column:

➤ It is hard to know when they have been achieved.

➤ It is hard to see how daily actions can make a difference – so we end up not taking those actions.

➤ It is easy to become demotivated and to give up as a result.

Take 'get fit for the summer' as an example. Perhaps I could walk up the stairs instead of taking the lift from now on. Would that get me fit? How will I know when I have achieved my goal? At what point will I feel 'fit'? Isn't it all relative?

By contrast, the more specific versions of the above goals on the right, bring certain *advantages*:

➤ It's easy to see exactly when they have been achieved. If I can do that mile in 10 minutes I've succeeded. If I can do it in 12 I'm on track. If it takes a couple of hours there's still work to be done!

➤ It's easier to see how small actions can make a difference. Because my goal is concrete, I can see how a small specific action like walking up the stairs is helping me towards it.

➤ It's easier to stay motivated as the goal approaches.

> **Case study:** John was the finance director of a national social housing charity. For some years the pressure to evaluate, measure and monitor outputs and outcomes had been inexorably increasing. Eventually, the only way he could get through all of the paperwork, statistical evaluations and reports was to work late regularly, take work home or work at the weekend. John didn't mind this too much, because he loved his work. 'However, I felt that the real victims were the family. Especially the kids. I seemed to be forever promising them that we'd do something together, or go somewhere and then backing out at the last minute in order to hit a work deadline. I was always promising them that we'd do it next week, and promising myself that I'd make more of an effort for them when we got over this busy patch...' But of course the busy 'patch' never seemed to end. John's solution was to make a specific commitment to take his two boys swimming on Saturday mornings. Now nothing is allowed to get in the way. 'Because the commitment was specific, it was much easier to keep to. Of course keeping the housing corporation happy is important; but not as important as keeping my family happy.' Who would disagree?

Measurable

We need to be able to monitor progress towards our goal if we are to recognise whether we are on, or off track, at any particular time.

> **Case study:** Viv had missed out on further education first time around. Although very bright, she had chosen to go straight into work at 16, whereas most of her friends went on to university. This never ceased to be a source of regret, but it was years before she felt ready to go back to college. Her ambition was to work as a probation officer. However, in order to qualify, she had first to get a degree. In order to get a place on a Sociology degree course she had to complete a foundation year. In order to get on the foundation year she needed to gain GCSE Maths. In order to pay for these courses, she needed to save up.
>
> Thus began a four-year programme with three phases, first to save up the cash to see her through her student days, then to get each of the two preliminary qualifications she needed. Then there followed three years at university. Was it worth it? 'That degree took six hard years, the first one scrimping, the next two holding down my job and studying in the evenings, and then the course itself.' said Viv. 'You have no idea how fantastic I feel to have stayed with it and achieved my goal. But with every stage completed, I knew I was on track. That helped me to keep going.'

Achievable

Our goals have to be realistic. For many years I wanted to run a deep sea research institute, cruising the Azores on my specially equipped yacht, swimming with dolphins and watching the sun set over a millpond ocean at the end of another day. Of course I was hopeless at biology at school and could scarcely tell one end of a boat from another, but apart from that there didn't seem to be any real obstacles! A distinction has to be made between *goals* and *wishes*. I was wishing that I was Jacques Cousteau, but that was never an achievable goal. So I went back to my values, which in this case are a love of nature, and adventure, and I found a way to manifest them within achievable goals. I was able, over a three-year period, to first qualify as a recreational SCUBA diver, gain experience in the North Sea and finally dive in the South China Sea with, if not dolphins, a truly astonishing procession of marine wildlife. If you stretch for something that is *just* beyond your reach then you will achieve it. If you do this often enough, you will achieve tremendous things by degrees.

Sometimes to be achievable, very large goals need to be broken down into 'sub-goals'. Nothing great is achieved in a single leap. Take the Apollo Moon Programme. In 1961 President Kennedy declared that by the end of the decade America would put a man on the moon and bring him safely home again. What was truly astonishing about this statement was that no one, not the scientists, the politicians, or the engineers who would form the team, had *even the slightest idea how it would be done*. Most of the technology didn't exist. The experience didn't exist (US astronauts had undertaken only 15 minutes of manned space flight). Only the imagination was in place. The way the Americans approached this most ambitious of goals was to break it down into a number of clear steps.

The Apollo Moon Programme

Step one was a successful manned orbital flight. This was achieved by John Glenn in February 1962.

Step two was to develop the procedures for manoeuvring and docking in space. This was achieved in the early 1960s by the Gemini astronauts.

Step three was to aim a projectile at the Moon and hit it. After several misses, Ranger 7 crashed into the Sea of Clouds on 31 July 1964.

Step four (achieved on 2 June 1966) was the first soft touch down, by the unmanned Surveyor 1, on the Moon's surface.

On 10 August 1966 *step five* was achieved with a successful unmanned orbit of the Moon and the identifiication of potential landing sites.

Step six was to send a manned craft to the Moon, put it into orbit and return it.

Step seven was the launch of the giant Saturn V booster rocket – the vehicle which would put the three-stage Apollo spacecraft into orbit around the Earth.

Step eight was a manned orbital flight around the Moon, achieved by James Lovell, Frank Borman and William Anders in Apollo 8.

Step nine was to send a manned craft to the Moon, put it into orbit and dispatch the lunar landing module, the *Eagle*, to the Moon's surface. So it was, that after trial runs and rehearsals of parts of the procedure by further Apollo missions, Neil Armstrong and Buzz Aldrin became the first men on the Moon on 20 July 1969.

The world remembers the moment when Armstrong spoke the historic words, 'Houston, Tranquillity Base here. The *Eagle* has landed'. But only those involved still remember the long haul. This particular 'overnight success' took eight years, cost twenty-five billion dollars, and tragically, a number of lives when three astronauts were killed by a fire as Apollo 1 prepared for take-off. But each day and each obstacle or error was seen as another step on a long journey. More critically, breaking the overall goal down into a number of constituent parts had a number of advantages:

➤ It prevented the team from feeling overwhelmed at the scale of what they were attempting.

➤ It allowed regular celebrations and congratulations as each step was achieved.

➤ It allowed the team to measure progress and remain motivated.

Relevant

Is the thing that we strive for the thing we really need? Or do we need to revisit our values and roles to seek an anchor? My advice would be to have at least some goals that reflect the values that are important to you and which redress any imbalances shown up when you considered your values earlier. Do you need to spend more time with your family, or do you need to earn more money? Do you want to stimulate your intellectual development by returning to education? Goals should be relevant to who we really are. They should not necessarily be about what others expect of us. It's your life. Make sure your goals are relevant to your needs and priorities.

Time based

We need to give ourselves a realistic timeframe in which to achieve our goals. In many ways there are no such things as unattainable goals – just unrealistic deadlines. If deadlines are too short, we are likely to find that we are slipping; too long and we'll find it easy to delay. So rather than say, 'we want to get fit and we'll know that we are there because we can run a mile in 10 minutes', we really need to say, 'we want to get fit for the summer and we intend to be able to run that mile in 10 minutes by the end of May'. Some very large goals may take a number of years to achieve. Others can be achieved within weeks or months.

4 Goals should be abundant

Life is a great big canvas, and you should throw all of the paint on it you can.

Danny Kaye

The more goals you have, the greater your chances of goal achievement. When setting goals, you should be prolific. Make a long list and don't worry if you feel you can't possibly achieve them all. The purpose is not to achieve everything on the list, but to give free flow to your thoughts, feelings, ambition and imagination. Once you have comprehensively described your potential future achievements, it is time to prioritise.

5 Goals should be prioritised

Gain clarity over the relative importance to you of the goals on your list, and then focus on those that would make the greatest difference. It's not much good looking back over a year of goal pursuit and realising that you managed the easy ones, but that they didn't really impact in any meaningful way on your levels of satisfaction and happiness. It's the big prizes that count.

6 Goals should be dynamic

The world, your circumstances, even your views, opinions and beliefs – these are all constantly changing. Our lives are *dynamic*. We constantly react to and interact with other people and chance events – we make decisions, suffer fortune (good or bad) and chart a course through life as a result. Every day may bring the possibility of a new perspective on your own, or someone else's character, the discovery of a hitherto unknown fact, the possibility of a promotion, a new role, fresh ideas or suggestions. Any one of these may open doors or close them, excite you or dismay you, lead to threat or opportunity.

Our goals should be flexible, dynamic, and as a result subject to change. Setting a goal is not a device to wed you inexorably to an unalterable course. It is a way of making sure that your current needs, desires and preferences are being served by your current daily activity, choices and priorities. So your goals should be regularly reassessed and then confirmed, modified or dropped according to what you currently think and feel. Once a month is probably often enough to undertake this assessment exercise. If the goals you made six months ago still matter today, then they are more likely to be genuinely rooted in your roles and values. Regular reassessment serves both to confirm that the goals you are striving for are the right ones, and to keep them at the front of your mind, to keep you focused and mindful that you should be acting today, not tomorrow, to bring their achievement closer.

7 Goals should be Big! They should address your dreams

If you only look at what is, you might never attain what could be.

Anonymous

It's difficult to know what our true potential is because it is just that – potential. By definition we haven't achieved it yet. And until we try, we'll never know if a particular goal is within our grasp. But this much is certain, if you aim low, you'll stay low. The challenge in aiming high is to see ourselves as more accomplished and successful than we currently are, to free ourselves of the constraints of our self image. That's what Muhammad Ali meant when he said 'The man who has no imagination has no wings.' But think about it! What were you like ten or even five years ago? Do you have more responsibility, Are you wiser and more respected in a way that you couldn't possible have imagined back then? As you grow, you become more experienced and more capable. Isn't it possible, then, that you haven't reached your limits, and don't know when, if ever, you will? Doesn't it therefore make more sense to resist the temptation to set limits prescribed by who you are today? It is the person of tomorrow that we're talking about.

8 Goals should be achieved step by step

A journey of a thousand miles must be begun with a single step.

Lao Tzu, circa 530 BC

Consider the massive, cumulative power of repeated, long-term, consistent action. The bigger and more ambitious the goal, the more we need to think about creating a programme, or project plan of small steps. Get into the habit of asking yourself 'how can I bring my goal closer by taking action today'. When athletes complete a competition they don't hang around a couple of months before thinking about beginning to train for the next competition. They begin a programme the next day. British distance runner Paula Radcliffe was asked soon after winning the 5,000 metres gold medal at the 2002 Commonwealth Games when she would begin to plan the next big challenge, the European Championships in Munich the following month. She replied that her thoughts had already turned to this competition on her lap of honour following the Commonwealth victory! Weight loss programmes work best if they don't rely on the crash philosophy, but aim for a little at a time. And your goals will have a much greater chance of success if you move towards them one step at a time. Whether you want to compete in the 100 metres at the next Olympic Games or simply write a great business plan, this approach will provide rich dividends. Even the biggest and most ambitious projects can be completed if you give them enough lead time, and you bring patience and persistence to the task. 'The best thing about the future is that it comes one day at a time.' (Abraham Lincoln)

Just as very few people are an overnight success, no one is an overnight failure. Failure comes from the consistent long-term repeated failure to take the action you need to bring your goals closer. Most failure is not about the spectacular crash. It is about a slow withering on the vine. Think about your regrets. Don't they tend to be about the things you haven't done, rather than the things you have done? Regrets more often come from inaction, rather than from action. As Mark Twain said, 'twenty years from now you will be more disappointed by the things that you didn't do than by the ones you did do'.

So, now you've had a chance to think about your values, roles and the characteristics of goals, it is time to embark on the goal programme. The first step is to write them down.

The goal programme

Use the following exercises to design your goal programme.

Step 1: write down your goals

Remember the rules:

➤ Link your goals to the *roles* you identified earlier.

➤ Focus where you want to achieve more or make big changes in your life. Allow your earlier thinking on *values* to guide you in this.

➤ Be *prolific*; come up with lots of goals, you can prioritise them later.

➤ Make sure that the goals you record are *SMART*.

➤ If you think the goals will take more than about 12 to 18 months to achieve, think about breaking them down into 'sub-goals'.

Your goal programme

Complete this chart by setting yourself goals linked to each of your roles. Don't feel you are limited to five roles — fill in as many as are relevant to you.

Role 1   **Goals/sub-goals**

_____   _____

                                              _____

                                              _____

                                              _____

                                              _____

Role 2   **Goals/sub-goals**

_____   _____

                                              _____

                                              _____

                                              _____

                                              _____

Your goal programme (cont.)

Role 3   **Goals/sub-goals**

_____   _____

                                                      _____

                                                      _____

                                                      _____

Role 4   **Goals/sub-goals**

_____   _____

                                                      _____

                                                      _____

                                                      _____

Role 5   **Goals/sub-goals**

_____   _____

                                                      _____

                                                      _____

                                                      _____

Step 2: prioritise your goals

There's little point in achieving goals that are relatively less important if that
means that the big prizes, the goals that will make a real difference, elude you.
So focus on the areas of most significance. Time management guru Alan Lakein

suggests that we call our most important goals our 'A' goals and then further prioritise them into A1, A2, A3, with A1 representing the highest priority and so on. I have adapted Lakein's technique into what I call the golden goal method. Simply take your top ten most important goals from the list you've generated above. Summarise them in the space below. These are your golden goals – those that are most important and would make the biggest difference to you. Then rank these golden goals into order of preference. This way, if you only achieve three things, you will have guaranteed that they will be the three things that are most important to you. If you only achieve *one* of your goals, it will be the one thing that will make most difference.

Golden goals

Goal	Priority
_____	☐
_____	☐
_____	☐
_____	☐
_____	☐
_____	☐
_____	☐
_____	☐
_____	☐

Now you know where your primary focus should lie over the coming days, weeks and months. You may still have the opportunity to achieve some of the goals at the bottom of your list. But what is particularly important is the fact that this process helps you to clarify what you really want, which goals will give most satisfaction, which will make a real difference. In the subsequent chapters of this book, I'll show you how to organise effectively to achieve them.

Summary:
clarify what you want from life and work

1 In order to establish a clear personal direction, you need to decide on three things:

> ➤ the *roles* you play in life
> ➤ the *values* that you have
> ➤ your *goals*.

2 Clarity on all these points will give you a very clear personal direction. People who have worked hard to identify and clarify their roles, values and goals know who they are, what they want and how they intend to achieve it. They might be said to have a clear and powerful personal vision.

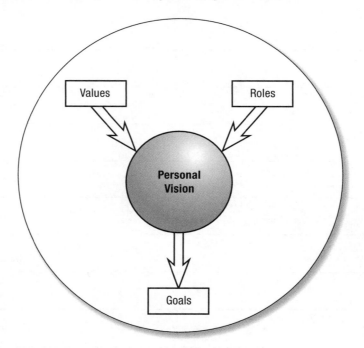

3 Roles, values and goals are interdependent. They are the three central pillars of personal planning, and if any are missing, or incomplete, it will be very difficult to come up with plans which will result in personal happiness, fulfilment and satisfaction. If they are all there, you are well on your way to creating a programme for real achievement in those areas which really matter to you.

4 If we think small, we'll achieve small. We can all achieve anything we want to, if we want it enough, have a clear and SMART programme and bring commitment and passion to the task (which is easy if it sits well with your most important roles and is fed by your values).

5   Apply a reality check. Go back and remind yourself of your most important
    role and your most important value base. Now look at your most important
    goal. Does the latter support the former? If yes, then you have already begun
    to plan a future that is consistent with the real you, to aim for achievements
    which will nourish your sense of self and give you a deep satisfaction on their
    completion. If there is dissonance between your goal and your roles and
    values, you may need to revisit your goal analysis and think again about
    the priorities!

Principle 2 Focus ...

... on activities which make a real difference

Overview

By the end of this chapter you will:

➤ have examined a number of techniques which put the emphasis on results, rather than activity

➤ have developed strategies to help you prioritise and plan effectively

➤ understand why urgent doesn't always mean important – and what to do about this

➤ focus on activities today which prevent crises tomorrow

➤ be able to shed up to 20 % of your current tasks, without any loss of effectiveness.

What do we mean by focus?

In the last chapter you established your goals. These are the outcomes, the results you want to see in your life. Think of your goals as the destination you want to get to. The journey that will help you arrive there is made up of the individual activities that fill your day. If you include in your day the tasks you must accomplish to make the goals materialise, then you are on the right track. If your day is filled with tasks which do not help you achieve your goals, then you might think of these as detours, wrong turnings and blind alleys.

A typical day will be full of demands, tasks and activities. Some of these will give you great results and represent time well spent. Others will deliver less. The 80/20 Principle (also known as the Pareto Principle after its originator, the nineteenth century Italian economist Vilfredo Pareto) states that a relatively small proportion of all of your endeavour (about 20 %) will deliver the vast majority of the results and successes you want. The other 80 % your time will be wasted on less than fruitful activities.

In his book, *The 80/20 Principle*, business writer Richard Koch says '80 % of what you achieve in your job comes from 20 % of the time spent'. In fact, recent studies in the United States suggest that workers spend up to three hours in any given day being *distracted* away from the key tasks for which they are employed. Inappropriate meetings, frustrating travel, time-stealing trivia – all of these things contribute to a massive time drain. If your experience in any way reflects this, it will have a massive negative impact on your personal effectiveness. Think about it. Three wasted hours per day is equal to around 100 *days* not really working, or at best getting very poor results, every year. Imagine how much more you could achieve if you could concentrate on the vital few activities which truly impact on your goals. Imagine what you could do if you reclaimed some of those hundred lost days! That's what we mean by 'focus' – and this chapter will demonstrate how to do it.

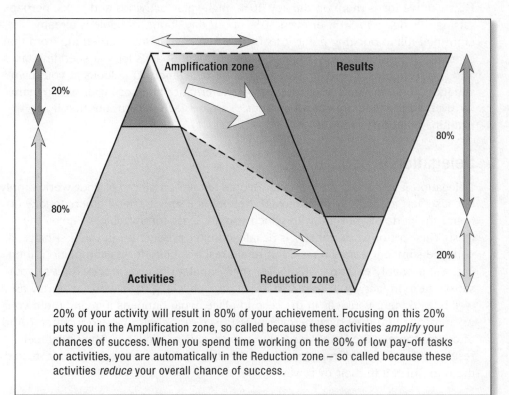

20% of your activity will result in 80% of your achievement. Focusing on this 20% puts you in the Amplification zone, so called because these activities *amplify* your chances of success. When you spend time working on the 80% of low pay-off tasks or activities, you are automatically in the Reduction zone – so called because these activities *reduce* your overall chance of success.

How to stay focused

In this chapter I want to look at three key techniques to help you retain the focus you need to achieve your goals. These are:

1 delegating non-essential commitments;

2 concentrating on 'important' over 'urgent' matters;

3 actively making time for your goals.

Each technique is free standing, which means that you can choose the one(s) you are most comfortable with or which fit your personal circumstances the best. However the more of these you can build into your daily approaches, the more you will benefit. Each of the techniques is aimed at eliminating detours and dead ends from your schedule, to allow you to take the repeated and determined daily action to achieve your most ambitious goals.

Focusing technique 1: delegating non-essential commitments

How can we focus more on the key 20%, high-value activities and tasks, perhaps raising this figure to 30% or even 40% of our day, if our schedule is already crammed full to bursting point? Clearly, we first have to lose something from that schedule. Prioritising always means de-prioritising! So let's look at shedding tasks and commitments. There are two models for delegation. One looks at your own situation; another looks at using this tool systematically across your whole team (or even your whole organisation). Let's examine each in turn, but first let's examine what delegation is not!

Delegation is not...

Delegation is *not* about asking other people to take on pieces of your work simply because you're too busy or stretched. Neither is it about asking others to take on board the parts of your job with which you are least comfortable, or enjoy the least. This sort of work transfer is usually counter productive. In the first place, if you give someone else the task, but retain responsibility for its completion, then you will probably end up looking over their shoulder to ensure they do it to your satisfaction. In fact you'll spend so much time checking their work, you may as well have done it yourself! In the second place, what happens if giving them your work means that they become over pressurised, and their own work suffers? And of course there is the longer-term damage to your relationship. They may feel resentful that you've dumped work on them, or hurt because you haven't trusted them to finish it in their own way.

Bubble delegation

This type of delegation effectively only involves two people, the delegator and the delegatee. They exist in a sort of 'bubble' where one delegates tasks to the other and the process stops there.

Delegation within the bubble becomes appropriate when:

➤ you have more important things to focus on;

➤ you can be reasonably sure that the task will be dealt with effectively if you delegate it;

➤ you'd like to stretch staff for whom you are responsible and increase their competence.

This last point is important. Delegation can be a great people development tool. By entrusting a junior member of staff with a project which will challenge them, you help them move a step closer towards realising their potential. As Goethe said 'Treat people as if they were what they ought to be, and you help them to become what they are capable of becoming'.

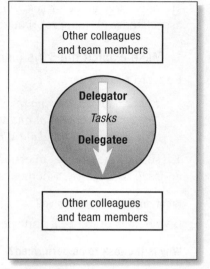

The advantages of delegation

➤ You will be freed up to deal with the genuinely important stuff.

➤ It's a great developmental tool to raise the skills and competencies of staff below you.

➤ More team members will be able to cover for one another in the event of staff shortage or illness.

➤ Several heads are better than one. Problems get tackled from more than one direction.

➤ When people are challenged, and succeed, they are much more likely to experience job satisfaction. Commitment and loyalty will grow as a result.

➤ It encourages exchange of ideas and communication.

➤ It shows your people that you value and trust them.

How to delegate using the bubble technique

There are five golden rules, which if adhered to, will prevent many problems associated with inappropriate delegation.

1 Make explicit the 5 Ws (and an H)

Rudyard Kipling said:

> I have 6 honest serving men, they taught me all I knew,
> Their names are What and Why and When,
> And Where and How and Who.

These six fundamental questions cover everything it's possible to ask about an issue: what, why, when, where, how and who.

What does the task involve?

Give details of the task and specify the results you need.

Why is the task to be performed?

You should be clear why you are undertaking something. If you're not clear why a certain meeting must be attended or task completed, don't delegate it, just dump it! If you are clear, explain this to the delegatee. Make plain the need and relative importance of the task.

When is the task to be completed by?

Give *reasonable* deadlines and expect the delegatee to stick to them. When setting the deadline, remember to take into account their current workload and the relative urgency and importance of the things already in their schedule. Allow for reasonable delays.

Where is the task to be completed?

Can the member of staff complete this from their own workstation or will some travel to another location be involved? If so, how will this impact on their other commitments?

Who is responsible?

With some tasks the delegatee may be able to take full responsibility and you need never hear about this again. With others, you may need to retain an overview and overall responsibility, in which case they will need to report back to you.

How is the task to be performed?

If part of your purpose is to stretch your people, it may be that they haven't attempted anything like this before. In this case you need to explain carefully and in detail how you suggest they do the job. Be as clear as possible. Offer training, mentoring or coaching support as appropriate. Specify the quality of the work which must be achieved. Give practical examples to demonstrate your point.

2 Write down the task and clarify the picture

If you ask someone whether they understand something, they are likely to say 'yes' – whether they fully understand or not. A better question is, 'explain to me what I've just asked you to do'. This is almost guaranteed to weed out any flaws in their understanding or identify areas where you have not explained clearly enough. Once you have reached full clarity and agreement, write it down as a sort of contract to which both parties can refer if any confusion creeps in later.

3 Agree a monitoring and evaluation procedure

You will need to be clear on the frequency of contact and the form of contact. The delegatee doesn't want to feel that you are breathing down their neck and you don't want to feel completely out of the loop, particularly if the project is an important one. At the same time remember that the whole point of this exercise is to put some distance between you and the work! So structure a clear schedule of contact and agree whether this needs to be face to face, by phone or e-mail, or by written report.

4 Be firm

You have an agreement which spells out purpose, method, outcome and timeframe. Stick to it and expect the delegatee to do the same. Don't accept shoddy work, or work that is half completed by the deadline. If they encounter problems, remind them that they are responsible for the results of the work, not just the work itself – encourage them to come up with suggestions and solutions. Don't allow them to delegate the problem back upwards to you.

5 Be supportive

At the same time as being firm, you need to be supportive. It's their first time. They may make mistakes. Accept this and expect errors. Mistakes are a vital part of learning. See the errors as valuable lessons and give them an opportunity to put them right. Being supportive includes offering the training or coaching support referred to earlier. And it includes giving appropriate praise and recognition when they accomplish a challenging task for the first time.

All of this will of course take time – and you may feel that you may as well have done the task yourself. But think of it this way. The time you spend now is an investment. The second and subesequent times your delegatee undertakes this task, they won't need such close support. So in the long run, you will save considerable amounts of time.

Why don't we delegate more regularly?

More often than not the reasons lie in our attitudes.

Common reasons not to delegate include...	and the reality
A fear of losing control.	If you're overworked and under pressure you're not in control. Delegation frees you up and gives you control.
'We've always done it this way' Habits, even bad habits, are hard to kick.	There is always a better process.
A perception that the people below us in the organisation do not have our experience, talent, or skills.	Delegation is a way to develop those skills and give them the experience.
A fear that we may not be considered so indispensable.	We're not indispensable. When we are ill the work goes on. When we retire the organisation will go on. When we die, life will go on. Get over it.
They may not do good work.	If you are under pressure, you're probably not delivering as well as you would like anyway. Plus, if you select those tasks that are relatively less important, what's the worst that could happen?
It will take too long to organise and manage.	Think of it as an investment. An initial investment of time will pay you dividends later when your subordinate is up to speed and operating effectively, freeing you up.

Blow some delegation bubbles

In the space below identify some of the tasks you feel you could delegate within the bubble. Under 'Strategy', identify potential individuals to whom you could delegate and think about how to apply the golden rules.

Task	Strategy
_____	_____
_____	_____
_____	_____
_____	_____
_____	_____
_____	_____
_____	_____

Structural delegation

One potential challenge with bubble delegation as described above is that it may be good for the delegator, but what if it simply leads to increased workload for the delegatee? Wouldn't it be better to have a system that allowed them to apply the same logic and rules, to free up some space in *their* already busy schedule, in order to take on the tasks delegated from above? That's what structural delegation is. It is a delegating process which involves the entire team, department or even organisation. This is a systematic process to ensure that every member of a team or organisation is able to shed those tasks that would be more appropriately completed by someone else. The key to this is the term 'more appropriately'. We need a way of identifying clearly whether going to the funding meeting is more appropriately a task for the director or the fundraiser. Is showing visitors around the centre more appropriately a task for the public relations assistant or the receptionist? Is filling in financial returns to statutory regulatory bodies like the housing corporation or the Charity Commission the job of the finance officer or the administrator? To be clear on issues like this we need to take three steps:

1 Ask 'what am I FOR?'

FOR stands for **F**undamental **O**utcome **R**equirement. Put simply, this means why are you employed? What are the bottom line results required by your employer? James Noon, author of *A Time* asks 'what unique contribution does (your) job make?' If you are a line manager your job description may include something like 'conduct appraisals', but the underlying purpose is to 'ensure a harmonious and functioning staff team'. In the box below establish your own outcome statement. It may be very straightforward. A fundraiser's FOR may be to 'raise £100,000 over the next 12 months'. A visiting service manager's FOR might be to 'ensure that 300 older people receive befriending visits over the next year, and that this service runs smoothly'.

Fundamental

Outcome

Requirement

What are you FOR?

> The outcomes attached to my post which must be achieved are:

2 Establish your critical priorities

These are the tasks for which you are responsible that are vital to achieving these outcomes. They are the parts of the job that achieve maximum return in achieving your fundamental outcomes.

My critical priorities (those things that most directly help me achieve my FOR) are:

_____

_____

_____

_____

_____

3 Look at the remaining priorities on your list

Is it possible to assign them to other team or department members for whom they'd be more appropriate, in terms of the outcomes *they* are employed to achieve?

Other tasks (minimal impact on my FOR)

_____

_____

_____

_____

_____

This process works best if it is carried out across a department, project team or working group. Each of your colleagues should therefore also complete the three steps. What happens is that tasks are cascaded as managers agree to shuffle activities and match them up with the outcome statements that have been agreed.

Case study: One practical way of achieving was attempted by Alistair, the manager of a busy community centre on an inner city estate. He wanted to reassess exactly where the members of his team should be focusing, while at the same time making sure everyone's area of focus fitted into an overall plan. He began by writing each person's FOR statement on an A4 envelope and sticking these all on the wall, side by side. Next he took a stack of postcards and got everyone in the team to record the elements of their job description or task list – one item per card, together with a rough estimate of how much time they spent per week on this particular task. When they were finished each card looked a bit like this:

> **Job element:** Attending partnership meetings
>
> **Time spent:** 2 hours per week

The flash cards broke down everyone's role into constituent parts. Alistair arranged to have all the cards typed so that it became a little harder to identify the person (via their handwriting) who currently had responsibility for each task or activity.

Then, as a team, Alistair's team mixed all of the flash cards up on a big table and started to sort them out logically. Together they decided which cards should go into which envelope. The sole criterion they applied was, 'will this task significantly help achieve the FOR statement on the envelope. When they were finished the contents of each envelope was used to rewrite people's job descriptions. 'The concrete result was that people found that they had lost lots of tasks, meetings, activities and responsibilities which did not help much towards their core job purpose' said Alistair. 'Of course, they found that many of these had been replaced by others, but these were parts of the job that they really should have been doing more of anyway.'

What will this process achieve?

Effective delegation on this model can have a very positive effect if it is carefully thought through. For example:

> The thinking will result in a wide-ranging and critical analysis of tasks, focus and responsibilities within teams, project groups or organisations.

> You are likely to find that a number of the flash cards are left over at the end. These tasks do not significantly help anyone achieve their FOR. Consider throwing them away and stop spending time on these low-return activities.

> Everyone in the team should find that they are able to reassign the tasks that do not help them do their job. They can fill this space with activities that *will* help them. They will become more effective.

> Everyone will have a much clearer idea of why they undertake activities. And they will understand that it is results, not activities, that count in the end. They may even get into the habit of asking 'why?' when they are asked to take on a new responsibility.

> You wouldn't expect a chief executive to do their own filing – it would make no sense to pay them the top salary in the organisation to use their time in this way. Every task should be completed at the lowest executive level possible in an organisation. This cascade principle works right across the board. The workload structure that will result from the above exercise will be more cost effective for the organisation, as many tasks will tend to be delegated downwards.

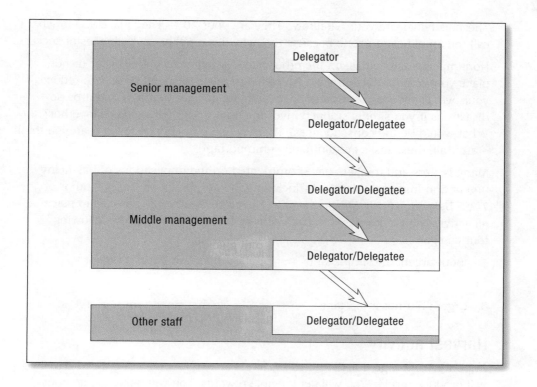

> Because this process is about *permanently* reassigning tasks, responsibility for completion and authority to act will be transferred along with the task itself. Ownership of the results of the activity, as well as the activity itself, is also transferred. You don't ever have to think about it again, whereas with conventional delegation you constantly worry about whether the task is being completed on time and up to quality.

> The process will help you find your 20% (according to the Pareto Principle) and increase your capacity to spend more time working on these critical tasks.

Focusing technique 2: understanding the difference between 'urgency' and 'importance'

There are two dimensions to any task. A task may or may not be *urgent*. If it is not, it can wait. If it is, we tend to react. When a phone rings it is answered. When a deadline looms, we work late.

A task may or may not be *important*. If it isn't, it doesn't matter if we fail to undertake it. If it is important, completing it can make a big difference to how much we achieve. Important activities tend to move you towards your key goals.

These activities are your 'vital few'. They are your 20%. They place you in what I call the amplification zone because the activities amplify your chances of success.

Non-important activities, on the other hand, whether they are urgent or not, place you in the reduction zone (so called because to spend time here reduces your overall chances of success or meaningful achievement). Would it be so disastrous if you simply stopped investing time in these activities altogether? What would be the consequences? There would probably be fewer than you think – after all, these tasks are ultimately unimportant!

Many writers and thinkers have commented on the implications of balancing urgent and important demands, including, notably, Stephen Covey, author of *The 7 Habits of Highly Effective People*. He suggests that it is possible to place all activities on a matrix, with each activity falling into one of the following four categories:

1   Both urgent and important   2   Important but not urgent

3   Urgent but not important   4   Neither important nor urgent

Harvest activity

Important and urgent activity I call 'harvest activity'. Completing these activities will produce results. You will get tangible rewards. You will harvest outcomes thick and fast. Examples of this type of activity include:

➤ the roadside rescue mechanic who fixes your car on the hard shoulder of the M25;

➤ the triage nurse who sutures a wound;

➤ the charity administrator who puts in a major grant application by the deadline.

All these people are getting the results for which they are employed. They are accomplishing their FORs. Their work is focused on the core purpose of their job. Activity that is both urgent and important will always move you towards your goals in meaningful ways.

There is however, a downside to harvest activity. Harvesting is back-breaking work. And as any farmer will tell you, you can't continually work a piece of arable land without exhausting its fertility. Because harvest tasks are urgent, with rapidly approaching deadlines, and because it is important that they are done well, the inevitable result is cumulative stress. And too much stress, as we shall see in chapter 7, is bad. Important questions to ask therefore are:

➤ how much of your job is made up of harvest activities?

➤ are you being damaged by the unrelenting pressure?

URGENCY

High   Low

IMPORTANCE

High

Both important and urgent	**Important but not urgent**
Urgent but not important	**Neither urgent nor important**

Low

Futile activity

Urgent but not important activity I call 'futile activity'. Sometimes it is hard to separate the immediately urgent from the ultimately important (the thesaurus function of my computer's spellcheck actually equates urgency with importance!) Some things seem as if they need doing *now* but actually make little difference to the world once they are done. Activities which fit in this category are phantoms. They fly at us and scream out their urgency and this helps them *seem* urgent and important – but if we ignore them, bad things rarely happen. A heavy smoker will feel a deep and urgent need to have a cigarette and will feel immediately better for it. But is smoking important to them in the long term? It may be that the newsletter article that you've promised a colleague is due. She says it's urgent. But is it important? If your job title is information officer, probably; but if it is senior drugs worker or counsellor – probably not! Futile activities keep you busy, but they don't move you towards your goals. They don't help you achieve your FORs.

Achievement activities

Important but not urgent activity is what I call 'achievement activity'. This is the most important type of activity. In this box within the matrix you would place all those activities which bring your goals closer, but which are also strategic and developmental. Planning, reflection and thinking go in here, as do activities which build and strengthen important relationships, personal or professional. Activities which will solve problems before they become a crisis – even before they arise go in this category. Examples of activities which fit well in this square include:

> ➤ undertaking a structural delegation exercise with your colleagues;
> ➤ spending adequate time with your loved ones;
> ➤ investing in an awayday with staff, trustees and other stakeholders to clarify the mission as a basis for building the business plan;
> ➤ signing up for an evening class to increase your skills;
> ➤ reading this book.

If none of the above, or activities like them, happen today or this week it's probably not the end of the world. But if they never happen, then that is an issue. And if you didn't have time this week, why should next week be any different? You may be accomplishing a lot by completing harvest activities but the question is, in the midst of all of the frantic busy-ness, if you don't have time to reflect and plan, how do you know that you're still on course, that you are concentrating on the right goals?

Waste activities

These are neither important nor urgent. You don't need to undertake these tasks. No one else needs you to undertake these tasks. This is time that is simply wasted.

It's up to you to choose how your day is structured. Will it be characterised by sustained intense pressure, by futile and ineffectual activity, by hiding from the pressure behind inconsequential tasks? Or will it contain quality time which helps you *plan* effectively, *prepare* for future challenges and *prevent* damaging behaviours or situations arising?

There is no one activity structure which is good for everyone. But there are a few common principles that probably do apply to most of us:

➤ We should be prepared, in a modern busy work environment, to spend time on urgent and important harvest activities if we want to gain results and make a difference. However too much time concentrating here will lead to increasing levels of stress and will eventually contribute to burn-out.

➤ Futile activities, those that are urgent but not important, should be avoided wherever possible.

➤ The same goes for waste activities. A little time wasting time is not so bad, as long as you've made a conscious choice to act in this way and you understand the consequences. Sometimes we all need to watch pulp TV, and that's fine. But too much time undertaking waste activities will create future stresses. Too much time wasted today will mean too much pressure tomorrow.

➤ Usually when we have to choose between something which is urgent but not important and important but not urgent, we focus on what is most immediate. Urgent tasks are loudmouthed and boorish. They shout at us and force us to focus on them. That's alright if they give you get a result. But if they don't...? It makes no sense to prioritise futile tasks over achievement tasks, but that is what sometimes happens.

To sum up, clearly things that are both urgent and important tend to come first, whilst things that are neither important nor urgent can largely be ignored with few repercussions. However when we are faced with a choice between something that is urgent, but not important (i.e. demands our immediate attention but does not contribute much to our core goals or purpose) and something which is important but not urgent (i.e. could contribute a lot to our goals, but can also wait) we tend to choose the former. And because our day is often filled with urgency, it means that each day we choose to put off the important stuff. The days become weeks, and the weeks become months. The urgency doesn't lessen and the activities which lead to the fulfilment of our goals are constantly put off.

Mapping your time

How much time do you spend on harvest, achievement, futile and waste activities?

On the matrix below, list the activities that you are engaged in during the course of a typical month, placing them in the appropriate box.

	High	**URGENCY**	Low
High	Both important and urgent (THE HARVEST SQUARE)	Important but not urgent (THE ACHIEVEMENT SQUARE)	
IMPORTANCE			
	Urgent but not important (THE FUTILITY SQUARE)	Neither urgent nor important (THE WASTE SQUARE)	
Low			

Changing your matrix spread

Now, in the space below, list items from your futility and waste squares that you think you can spend less time on. In the right-hand column, list achievement square activities which you can spend time on in their stead.

Futile or wasteful activity to lose	Time saved per week	New achievement activity to substitute

Case study: Tomas works as a policy officer for a major European foundation. He is extraordinarily busy, but has a family and believes that to work late regularly would be wrong. To prevent this he uses a phrase which he writes at the top of his to-do list at the beginning of every day. It reads:

'what one thing must I achieve today, to go home feeling satisfied and in control?'

This he calls making a 'results bargain' with himself. The deal is this. He has hundreds of things to do, a list as long as your arm – unless he is very careful he knows that he will end up staying late. As he becomes more tired he will become less effective. It's possible that he will go home feeling frustrated, exhausted and still have an enormous number of things to achieve tomorrow. What is important of course is not what he 'does' but what he 'achieves'. He needs to focus on the important at the expense of the urgent. And that is where the bargain comes in. By asking the question, Tomas is able to identify the activity or task which will make a difference. Get that done and it doesn't really matter whether or not he completes the rest of the tasks on his 'to-do' list. The result is he goes home on time, recuperates properly, arrives tomorrow refreshed and alert, and performs to his full potential. By asking the question every day, he gets cumulative outcomes of increased energy, greater achievement and he feels less overburdened and stressed. Of course many things don't get done as a result. But that's the point!

Focusing technique 3: actively make time for your goals

'Creating' time

Here are just two ways you can make more time to achieve your goals.

Watch less TV

In his novel *Brave New World*, Aldous Huxley describes a drug that is dispensed to the population to keep them passive. 'Soma' helps people feel happy, relaxed and calm. But it also prevents them from taking control, seeking change or actively engaging with what is important. Marx called religion the 'opiate of the masses' and he had much the same idea in mind. Today, we live with an opiate just as pervasive and powerful for many people as anything Marx or Huxley could have imagined – the TV. It has been estimated that by the time a child is six years old, he or she will have invested more time in watching TV than they will spend talking to their father during the course of the rest of their lives. If you watch only three hours of TV per day, that's over 1,000 hours per year. During the course of a working life, that's in the region of 6,000 working days spent glued to the telly. Just how many documentaries about sharks or home makeovers do you need?

Go home early

One implication of the Pareto Principle is that you should never take work home or work beyond the normal close of your regular office hours. You should never work in the evening or at weekends. 'Impossible!' you cry. 'If I didn't put in all of these extra hours, I'd never be able to cope'. And of course it does seem that way. However, the Pareto Principle is quite clear on this. You will do your best work in the 20 % or so of your time when you are fresh, alert and focused. For the rest of the day, you will get a diminishing scale of returns as you become more tired. Trying to finish work over the weekend simply means that you will be less effective on Monday morning, because you have not spent the time relaxing, recharging and refreshing yourself. Taking work home in the evening simply means that you will be tired tomorrow. And that means you'll be less effective. So you'll end up taking work home again. And so on and so forth. To break this cycle, simply stop. By using your spare time to recover from the challenges of a busy life, by recharging your batteries properly, you will find that you get more from your day. Use your time to work on your goals and personal projects and your employer will see a marked improvement in the thing they pay you to produce – quality.

What can you expect from these techniques?

I've helped hundreds of individuals use the techniques described in this chapter to focus on the activities which really make a difference, at the expense of those that steal their precious time. The regular feedback that I get suggests that using one of more of these techniques can help individuals to get rid of up to 20% of their workload, with no loss of focus on what is really important!

Summary:
focus on activities which make a real difference

1   The Pareto Principle suggests that 80% of what you achieve in your job will be delivered by 20% of the activities you undertake.

2   You can make enormous strides in productivity and effectiveness if you can identify this 20% and focus on it, at the expense of the other 80%.

3   Delegation 'in the bubble' not only frees you of some tasks, but can be a powerful development tool for your junior staff.

4   Structural delegation is a systematic process to ensure that every member of a team or organisation is able to shed permanently those tasks that would be more appropriately completed by someone else.

5   Everyone in your team or department should know what they are FOR and which tasks will deliver their key outcomes. They should focus on these at the expense of others.

6   Focusing on important over urgent activities will put you in the amplification zone, instead of the reduction zone. Remember that you have to make a conscious decision to focus on the important. In *First Things First*, Stephen Covey says 'Anything less than a conscious commitment to the important, is an unconscious commitment to the unimportant'.

7   You need to map your harvest, achievement, futile and waste activities. Then you need to stop getting involved in futile and waste activities, using the space created in your schedule to take on more achievement tasks.

8   Every hour you spend surfing TV is an hour lost that you never get back. Remember that 'you are a long time dead'.

9   If you are too busy, it's better to go home early than late.

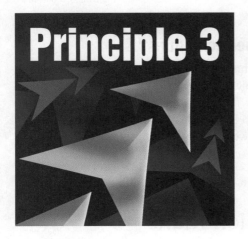

Principle 3 Structure ...

... your day for maximum effectiveness

Overview

By the end of this chapter you will be able to structure your day to deal with most of the common time management challenges. Specifically you will:

➤ gain control of your life, by controlling each and every day. You will have tools to help you with tactical prioritisation

➤ create schedules which allow you to get the most important work done, every time

➤ find the 'hidden hour' in every day to help take some of the pressure off

➤ be able to understand your own energy pattern, and use this information to undertake complex or important tasks at appropriate times.

Why do we need a structured approach to managing our time?

On the way to achieving your goals you will be faced with a sometimes bewildering array of daily choices. Should you go to the meeting or finish the report? Should you take work home this weekend or visit your family? Should you spend a morning working on the budget or catching up on background reading? As Thomas Carlyle said 'Nothing is more terrible than activity without insight'. This chapter is about gaining insight into what you should be doing at any time in your day.

Perhaps the only thing you know for sure is that you can't do it all. You have to decide where you will focus to get the best results, to make most progress towards your goals and to feel in control and as little stressed as possible. You have to be able to prioritise what gets done and what does not. But of course, this is not always as simple as it seems. How many times have you started a day with clarity about what needs doing; then, as the day progresses, it seems to spin increasingly out of control, until you are chasing your tail, running behind with your schedule? To get the control back, we need to think how we can effectively organise, or structure our day. A good structure to the day will help us make the right decisions.

Case study: Carole was the manager of a women's accommodation project in Wales which was undergoing an organisational review. This was a traumatic time for staff, and some of them were finding it hard to adjust to the changes in their role and routine. At the same time the review had led to a number of funding opportunities for new projects.

'I felt under enormous pressure. I was trying to offer close support to key staff in the shape of regular structured supervision sessions. I'm not usually at my best first thing in the morning, but it's the only time that all of the staff are in. We have 18 staff, so this was making a great demand on my time. At the same time, I wanted to bring in extra staff to ease the burden and to launch new projects, so I was researching and writing to lots of charitable trusts. I could usually find a couple of hours after lunch, when the office was relatively quiet, a couple of times a week to do this. Although, strictly speaking this wasn't on my job description, I knew that if we could just raise the money, then I'd be able to relax.'

Although supporting some staff with supervision was undoubtedly the right *thing* to do, was Carole doing it at the right *time*, when she 'wasn't at her best'? How much support can a manager offer when she herself is struggling to cope? Could Carole have scheduled better?

Although the important task of writing to trusts was clearly done at the right *time*, when the office was quiet and there would be few distractions, was raising money for new projects the right *thing* to be doing, when Carole had so many other demands on her time and the organisation had so many competing needs? Could Carole have prioritised better?

Capture everything that needs to be done

When faced with meetings, reports, spreadsheets, e-mails, crises, problems and all of the other things that a pressurised day can throw at us, we need a way of capturing and recording what needs to be done. Unless, like the proverbial elephant, we have the power never to forget, it makes sense to write tasks down somewhere. Some people use yellow sticky notes, others keep a desk diary or a wall planner. Some scribble notes on scraps of paper and stick them on a teller's spike. And others use a combination of these, or similar strategies.

> **Case study:** Pauline is a community arts worker in a vibrant theatre in Scotland. Increased funding and a new and dynamic director meant that she became significantly busier over about an 18-month period. To try and keep track, and to balance her competing work and home life, Pauline started a multiple notebook system.
>
> 'I kept a *blue* notebook for work. At the front I noted down everything I wanted to do and at the back I kept dates, times and notes. Also, I had a *green* notebook for personal tasks – the house and domestic matters, reminders to deal with school issues for the children, bills that needed to be paid, that sort of thing. And for myself, I kept a *yellow* notebook. This would include reminders and task lists to do with my social life, night classes, church commitments and so on. Eventually I found that I was spending so much time organising my system, cross referencing and double checking appointment times, tasks and reminders between books, that it began to seriously eat into the time I'd allocated to get things done! I also found I could never find the right notebook when I needed it.'

Clearly Pauline needed a simpler system. The last thing a busy person needs is something to cause more stress! The point of a daily management tool is to make things more straightforward, and for that to work we need to apply a couple of rules. These are:

➤ When you record what needs to be done, keep it simple. Just because our lives are complex doesn't mean that we need a complex tool to manage it. In fact the opposite is true. The simpler the better.

➤ Use only one list. You only have one life, so it makes sense to use one planning tool. If you have a handheld PC in your briefcase, an appointment book on your desk and a calendar on the fridge door, dates, appointments or notes are almost sure to disappear as you transfer them from one medium to another. Also, if you record your tasks in a number of places, you'll have difficulty keeping an overview, seeing the big picture. I recommend that you abandon any system which is multi-layered and use the good old to-do list.

To-do lists that don't work

Simply having a to-do list is not in itself enough to guarantee a day that is controlled and effective.

Case study: Mike was a development worker for a charity working with disadvantaged young people in Brighton. He had kept a to-do list for many years, but found the technique wanting. Here is a typical list as used by Mike:

1	Open post	10	Fill in expenses claim
2	File post	11	Press release
3	Reply to letters	12	Newsletter article
4	Organise diary	13	Staff meeting
5	Make conference arrangements	14	Order stationery
6	Appraisal meeting with Sue	15	Critical path analysis for project Y
7	Set up new computer	16	Prepare budget for next year
8	Evaluation report for project X	17	Funding applications
9	Meet with volunteers		

'I would start the day and feel quite intimidated by the number of things on the list. Sometimes I'd simply start at the top and see how far I could get by the end of the day – which, given the number of interruptions in my office, often wasn't very far. More often I'd look for the simple things and the quick things and do those first. So the sequence of activity would probably be 1) open post (put to one side on desk), 2) organise diary, 3) realise that I hadn't made conference arrangements so check train times, accommodation availability and make bookings, 4) fill in expenses claim form (always fun!), 5) attend staff meeting (unprepared for because of the rather hectic activity so far today) and 6) think about starting next year's budget, realise computer was still not set up, so order stationery instead.'

The net result of all of this activity? On one hand Mike completed more than a third of the items on his list. On the other hand, half the day had gone, he had been busy all morning without accomplishing any of the really important things (like completing funding applications). At the back of his mind he was aware that these needed to be done and the stress was steadily building. His office was messier than when he started, courtesy of the unfiled mail, and he faced more delay before he could get down to real work (the computer was still in its box). If this pattern is repeated day after day, the working environment soon becomes chaotic.

Mike's to-do list doesn't seem to be helping him much at all. However, the application of three simple rules could transform his list in terms of its power to assist him to function effectively and purposefully.

The three golden rules of the to-do list

A to-do list should be:

1 streamlined

2 goal focused, and most important of all

3 prioritised.

Rule 1: streamline your list

Don't include routine, or things scheduled to happen whether you make a choice or not. The purpose of the list is to prompt and guide you. If you get in to work and routinely check for e-mails at 8.55am, then you don't need this on a list. It just happens automatically. By eliminating routine things, you will bring down the numbers of tasks on the list, making it appear more manageable, and this in turn will help to motivate you. For example, I don't think Mike needs to put 'appraisal meeting with Sue' or 'Volunteers' meeting' on his list, because these will already be in the diary or schedule. He should, however, include any work that has to be done in support of these meetings. These are tasks that will need his decision, commitment and control. So including them on his to-do list would help him keep on track, plan when to undertake the work and retain control.

Rule 2: build a bridge to your key goals

If you think of your key goals as a 'wide angle' perspective on your life, then your to-do list is the zoom perspective. It includes the fine detail that will contribute to the broader picture. Your list should always include some activities, exercises or tasks which bring your goals closer.

Rule 3: prioritise the list

Most critical of all, we have to prioritise the tasks on our list, because there is always more work than time. I'd suggest you use the following criteria:

> the relative urgency of the task;

> the relative importance of the task (see chapter 2 for a more thorough examination of these key concepts);

> how much goal return does the task deliver? In other words, will the task help you towards any of your golden goals?

Simply consider these issues and then divide the list into three categories of relative priority. Why three? Simply because two is not enough and four is too many. Three seems to work just right. I once was told by a delegate on one of my courses that whilst working for the Civil Service she had been encouraged to have one list, with some tasks picked out as 'must do' tasks. But this didn't really reflect the subtleties of prioritising effectively. Within a few weeks members of her team had customised the system and had three levels of priority; the 'must do' priority, the 'must, must do' priority and the 'must, must, *must* do' priority!

Personally, I assign a colour to each of my categories, using highlighter pens. I like the idea of colour coding. Colours are symbolic. I use red, a warm, demanding, vibrant colour to signify my most urgent and important tasks, yellow to highlight those tasks which are relatively less important or urgent and blue, a cool colour, to show those tasks that have least priority. Or you may like to use the ABC principle. This means put an 'A' next to those tasks which are today's highest priority; a 'B' next to those that are of a second order of priority; and a 'C' next to those that, relatively, don't really matter that much.

It doesn't matter what system you use to flag up relative priority, as long as you are comfortable with it and use it systematically, every day.

'A' or 'red' tasks

These tasks are your major priority for the day. Either they need to be dealt with as a matter of some urgency, or they are developmental, helping you move a little closer to your key goals. There should be no more than two to three hours of 'red list' activity on your to-do list.

'B' or 'yellow' tasks

These tasks are relatively less urgent, less important, or less goal-focused than 'A' tasks, but still deliver some pay back. Or they may be important, but not as urgent as other tasks, which you have decided are red. Some yellow tasks will become tomorrow's red tasks.

'C' or 'blue' tasks

These tasks are relatively unimportant or non urgent. Or they may simply deliver nothing in terms of helping you achieve what you need to today.

Once you've done this, it becomes much easier to focus on the issues and activities which will help you to achieve. Your energy should be primarily focused on the red list within your overall to-do list.

Tasks you are given by others – red, yellow or blue?

Sometimes we are asked to take on jobs by other people. The best thing to do is say 'no' (see chapter 4) but sometimes circumstances mean the work ends up with us anyway. Part of the problem is deciding on the relative priority of those unwelcome tasks. The person who gives you the task is very unlikely to say 'Oh, anytime in the next 12 months is OK'. They are more likely to tell you that it is urgent, that the sky will fall in if it isn't completed on time, that nothing on God's earth is more important. Here's a simple way to determine how accurate these protestations are.

1 Do nothing. Simply wait.
2 If they send you an e-mail or a memo, it's probably a 'C' or blue task (lowest priority).
3 If they telephone, it's probably a 'B' or yellow task (medium priority).
4 If they knock on your door, it's an 'A' or red task (highest priority)!

Advantages of prioritised to-do lists

There are four main advantages to a prioritised to-do list.

You'll feel better about never finishing

Let's face it, it's a mug's game trying to finish a to-do list by close of play on Friday. Firstly, if you fail (and you usually do) then you go home feeling defeated by the pressure. And secondly, if you do finish, your boss is just likely to give you more to do!

Surely it makes more sense to go home at the end of the day feeling that you've done the meaningful things – that you have attacked the red list and won! Yes, there will be things left over, but if these are a few yellows and blues, then that's OK. The reds are all done!

You can negotiate tasks away

If your list shows that you have too many yellows or blues to deal with, you can use this as a basis for negotiation with your team leader or line manager. Surely it makes more sense for you to concentrate on those areas where you get real job results? Perhaps someone else can take on some of the yellows or blues; or indeed, can you simply ignore them? Would the world end if the blues didn't get done (given that you'll be achieving more red tasks as a result)?

You'll get back on track more quickly after interruptions

In chapter 4 we examine how to minimise interruptions. But it is unlikely that we will ever be able to eliminate them altogether. Indeed, interruptions form an inherent part of those jobs that are about supporting people, solving team problems, dealing with the enquiries from public or colleagues. They *are* going to happen and they *will* disrupt your flow. A prioritised to-do list is a sort of 'anchor'. It helps you to refocus, pick up where you left off and concentrate again on your key priorities. Without it, you may find that you get sidetracked, particularly if the interruption has been a long one, and get involved in any one of the other urgent tasks.

It will signal if you are genuinely overwhelmed

Sometimes we are simply given too much work. Perhaps you line manager is ill and you're acting up, but still have all of your old responsibilities as well, or perhaps your organisation has been restructured because of a funding cut, and a smaller team is trying to produce the same number of outcomes. Whatever the reason, you need to address the root cause, and that involves re-examining what is a realistic amount of work for one person to accomplish well, without danger of exhaustion or burn-out. A well-structured, prioritised list, that remains unmanageable, will signal this clearly.

The one-stage planning technique: turn your list into a schedule

Once you have prioritised your tasks, the next stage is to determine the most effective *time* to undertake them. Because these two stages, prioritisation and scheduling, are so closely linked, it makes sense to have one tool to undertake both. Your prioritised to-do list shouldn't be separate from your diary, but an integral part of it. The model page shown below demonstrates how Mike's to-do list (see page 57) could have worked, using this system.

Schedule		To-do tasks		
			Category	
9.00				
9.30				
10.00		Funding applications	A	✔
10.30	Appraisal meeting			
11.00	with Sue	Fill in expenses claim	B	
11.30		Critical path analysis for project Y	B	
12.00				
12.30		File post	A	✔
1.00		Set up computer	A	✔
1.30				
2.00		Evaluation report for project X	B	
2.30				
3.00	Staff meeting	Prepare budget for next year	A	✔
3.30		Conference arrangements	C	
4.00				
4.30		Reply to letters	B	
5.00				
5.30	Volunteers' meeting	Order stationery	C	
6.00		Newsletter article	C	
6.30				

As you can see, Mike has prioritised his work and is concentrating on the 'A' tasks. At the end of the day he will have the satisfaction of looking down his list of ticked items and know for sure that he focused in the right areas. Some of the routine tasks, like 'open post' have been streamlined away. The list is shorter than Mike's original.

He has taken the meetings from the list, and included them instead on the schedule. This shortens his list, but also makes clear how much free time he actually has to accomplish his 'A' tasks. He has three hours of meetings. If they finish on time he will have a maximum of four hours of available time in which to do other work. This gives Mike a clear idea of what is achievable. He has the option of downgrading some of his 'A' tasks to 'B' tasks until tomorrow or later in the week, if he feels that he simply can't achieve them.

To get the most from the one-stage planning system, you should stick to the following eight rules:

1   Use the 'popcorn technique'

2   Plan continually

3   Layer activities

4   Look for multi-achievement opportunities

5   Find your 'high energy window'

6   Use the 'hidden hour'

7   Break up big tasks into smaller ones

8   Use the 'switch technique'.

The popcorn technique

There can't be a crisis next week. My schedule is already full.

US diplomat, Henry Kissinger

Everyone knows that if you fill a bowl to the brim with popcorn and place it in the oven, the popcorn will explode out of the container. Popcorn always expands to take up twice as much space once you apply the heat. The only way to avoid a mess is to *half-fill the bowl*. When it emerges from the oven, you'll find that the popcorn has expanded to absorb all of the available space – but it will be contained within the bowl.

The same principle applies to your schedule. In a perfect world, we'd be able to accomplish an hour's worth of work in any given hour. But we don't live in a perfect world. To begin with we are likely to be interrupted. As we see in chapter 4, interruptions can add considerably to the length of time required to accomplish any task. It's also possible that we have underestimated the true 'time cost' of a task by leaving out the hidden time costs from our calculation. Typical time costs which people forget to account for include:

➤ travel time to and from appointments;

➤ setting up time for group activity;

➤ thinking and reflection time;

➤ revising time to do things again if the quality isn't right first time;

➤ recharging time – we can't go from one high energy project to another without some time to recuperate in between times; to attempt this is to set ourselves up to fail.

All of these elements are like heat being applied to popcorn. What we expect to take 'so much' space in our schedule, ends up taking much more. In fact, it seems to me that over the course of an entire day, things take about twice as long as we at first think. That's why I'm recommending that you only schedule in half of your available time. If you have a seven-hour working day, and you have two hours of meetings planned, then you have five hours of available time. You should, therefore schedule in around two, to two-and-a-half hours of 'A' priority tasks. They'll probably take the whole five hours to complete.

The advantage of operating this way is not that we get any more work done. It is simply that we set ourselves reasonable challenges which we then regularly overcome. And at a stroke, we go home at the end of every day as someone who has succeeded in reaching their workload goals, rather than as someone who feels the weight of failure and a backlog of unfinished and unstarted tasks.

Plan continually

> *Plans are nothing. Planning is everything.*

General Dwight D. Eisenhower

It's not the mechanical process of writing things down that brings us a clear perspective and a focused mind. It is the thinking that lies behind the process. In time planning terms, we need to get into the habit of scanning the horizon to spot obstacles, opportunities, pressures and deadlines as they approach, and before they are upon us, causing a crisis. For that reason I'd suggest a principle of continuous planning:

➤ Spend 10 to 15 minutes at the end of every day, planning tomorrow in *detail*. Carry forward any uncompleted tasks from your to-do list, add new items and then re-prioritise the whole list using the red/yellow/blue, A B C system, or any other system which clearly indicates three categories of relative priority.

➤ Spend 20 to 30 minutes at the end of the week planning the next week, using a little *less detail*. Be *broadly* aware how you will spend each day from Monday to Friday. Be aware of important meetings or other commitments for which you may have to prepare. Dedicate some specific time for high quality, uninterrupted work.

➤ Spend 30 minutes to one hour at the end of the month looking ahead and planning the coming month in *outline*. Keep an eye on approaching deadlines. Plan for any trips, including hotel and travel arrangements. Get a sense of how larger projects are going; are you on time and on budget? Do you need to change direction or take action? Use this time to reassess your goals. Confirm your golden goals and ask yourself, 'what can I do in the coming month to help realise these?'

Monthly planning is a little bit like going on a long trip. Before you set off you might get out the map, plot the route, check the weather forecast and maybe phone a motoring organisation to check for roadworks along your intended route. You don't need a serious amount of detail at this stage, just a broad understanding of what lies ahead.

Weekly planning is equivalent to driving along the motorway. Every so often you might need to check road signs, calculate distance to your destination, keep an eye on the petrol gauge. You need to exercise more attention to detail, but you are still largely thinking about what lies ahead, rather than what will happen in the immediate future.

Daily planning is similar to what you must do as you negotiate town traffic when you get close to your destination. At this stage you need a significant amount of clarity and detail about what lies immediately in the car's path. Pedestrians, other vehicles, tight bends and traffic lights all need instant reaction. This part of the process needs serious attention to detail.

The main advantages to this approach are:

➤ You get used to having an overview. Deadlines don't creep up, you are less likely to be surprised by developments. You get accustomed to looking ahead and monitoring what is approaching.

➤ You get closure on the day. By planning tomorrow today, you leave work with a very clear idea about the challenges that tomorrow will bring and how you plan to meet them. Because you are only scheduling 50% of your available time, you know when things will happen and that you have a good chance of staying in control and finishing on time. Because you have prioritised your to-do list, you know where you will focus. The net result is that you will experience the calm that comes with certainty.

Layer activities

I've met people who try to deal with an overwhelming to-do list by running a number of activities at once, or multi-tasking. Usually I wouldn't recommend this. Very few people can genuinely and effectively multi-task, that is simultaneously undertake parallel tasks without error. Computers yes – people very rarely. However, there are a few limited circumstances where it may be possible to get away with it. For example it might be possible to layer activities on other activities which are purely automatic, or 'no-brainers'. You could for example speak to friends or colleagues on the phone (using a cordless phone, headset or speaker) while you clean the house, or tidy your desk. You may catch up on reading while you travel by train or plane.

So you needn't rule out this tactic altogether, but be aware of its limitations. And consider that if you get into the habit of doing this (other than in the circumstances similar to those listed above), you may get more done in the short term, but in the long term you are more likely to feel stressed, stretched and exhausted.

Look for multi-achievement opportunities

Doing something that serves two purposes is not multi-tasking – it's multi-achieving. You may have a goal to get fit and a goal to spend more time with the kids. Taking them swimming serves both goals. That's good practice.

Find your high energy window

I used to work in a housing organisation with Brenda. She was most definitely not a 'mornings person'. In fact establishing eye contact with her before she'd had at least three cups of coffee was downright dangerous! By lunchtime she was 'coming around'. But by two in the afternoon she was really motoring. We all feel at our best at different points during the day. We each have an individual daily energy pattern which dictates the time of day when we are best equipped to take on the most challenging tasks. If you were to plot your energy pattern on a graph, it probably wouldn't look like a straight line or a smooth curve. Rather, a typical person's energy level tends to fluctuate up and down as the day progresses – perhaps you get an energy lull just before lunch, only to recover again once fuel is taken on board.

Problems arise when you have an important job to undertake which demands focus, concentration or creativity and one of the lulls hits home. Then it really is difficult to summon up the motivation to knuckle down and get the job done. At the same time, it's just as problematic to find that you are sitting in an undemanding meeting, when your energy is high, your mind alert and there are a hundred and one other things you could be doing.

The answer is to take control by:

➤ mapping your own energy pattern to discover your regular highs and lows;

➤ pro-actively scheduling in your most important or challenging work into the high energy windows that appear as part of your regular pattern;

➤ ensuring that you can focus during this time by removing the possibility of interruptions taking place.

This principle has been called a number of things over the years, from 'A time' to 'the golden hour' to 'prime time' and has been used extensively in the commercial and voluntary sectors in the US and in Europe. Usually, proponents will seek to close their door for the duration of the high energy window. I've heard it described as 'having a meeting with myself'. In other words, just as your colleagues wouldn't barge in on you if you were in the middle of an important meeting, so they should be discouraged from interrupting you during this key work time. I know of teams working in open plan environments who, unable to close an office door on the outside world, have purchased personal CD players with headphones to shut themselves off from the chatter, phones and other distractions whilst they are in this high performance zone.

The advantages of this approach are:

➤ It creates a sanctuary from the other pressures of the day and creates a place in your schedule where your most challenging tasks meet with the most capable 'you'.

➤ It ensures that you are doing the right thing at the right time, which as we discussed earlier, is the principle on which all effective time management is based.

➤ It ensures that you will make fewer mistakes on your most important projects or reports and that you will complete them more quickly than otherwise would have been the case.

➤ According to Carol Dudley, a trustee with Merton Family Centre, her regular use of the golden hour ensures that staff who might otherwise interrupt her work with an attempt to 'upwardly delegate' a problem, are forced to go off and solve it themselves. 'It is a great staff development tool' says Carol.

Case study: Martin is a training officer for a major UK educational charity. He works out of a busy open plan office in the North West. 'My best time is first thing in the morning. I've found two main disadvantages to arriving at 9.00am. Firstly, travelling in to work at that time puts me in the thick of the rush hour. Secondly, everyone else arrives then, and before I know it there are a hundred different distractions. So, these days my practice is to set off from home at 7.00am to arrive at 8.00am. Not only do I miss most of the traffic, but I then have one blissful hour to plan, reflect and do any really important stuff before the maelstrom of the day begins for real. The office is quiet, the phone never rings, I'm never interrupted. An added bonus is that I regularly build up enough lieu time to take a long weekend every two or three weeks. And this time I reserve for me!'

Use the hidden hour

One sunny afternoon not so long ago I was at the beach with my two young sons. I sat and watched as they had a race to fill their plastic buckets with pebbles. The older of the two swiftly grasped the way to easy victory. He looked for the largest stones he could find, so that the bucket would fill quickly. After a minute or two he was able to announce his triumph. The younger brother thought about this for a couple of seconds, examined his competitor's bucket carefully, and then announced (with some indignation) 'it's not really full. I can see gaps'. And of course he was right. The bucket was full of spaces between the stones. They started to pour sand into the bucket, which gradually filtered down to fill these spaces. At first glance the bucket had appeared full, but once you noticed the many gaps and spaces, it became clear that there was in fact quite a lot of space in there.

This is the idea behind the hidden hour – that there is a collection of small 'spaces', or pockets of time 'hidden' in the fabric of your schedule, which, when taken together, seem typically to add up to around one hour per day. The pockets lie, usually unnoticed, between our big 'pebbles' – the meetings, projects and reports that make up the bulk of our day. A typical hidden hour might be found secreted in spots such as these:

➤ waiting for your PC to boot up in the morning;

➤ standing by the kettle, waiting for it to boil;

➤ when you are ready to begin a meeting in your office a few minutes before everyone else arrives;

➤ when your energy levels dip slightly and you find yourself glancing through trade catalogues, shuffling papers, sharpening pencils, anything but turning to a more challenging task;

➤ when you have an out of office meeting and you arrive a few minutes earlier than planned;

➤ when you have a scheduled task, such as a staff supervision session, and your colleague is a few minutes late;

➤ When you try to make a phone call and the line is busy. You wait a few minutes before calling back.

How to use the hidden hour

> *We could all achieve great things if it wasn't for all the little things that get in our way.*
>
> Jean Paul Sartre

If you can get into the habit of spotting these empty spaces in your schedule, you can use them to undertake some of the blue, 'C' tasks, those low-grade, routine or boring tasks which otherwise might be left hanging around on your to-do list. For example, bits of filing, reading, passing on information, e-mails or calls which are neither urgent nor important but which you would like to make.

The first step is to identify appropriate 'C' tasks that can be picked up and removed from your list. I put mine on a separate page in my planner, which sits just behind the main list. I choose those tasks that fit a certain profile. Specifically they have to:

➤ Be do-able in 5/10 minutes. This means I can pick one up and 'insert' it into one of the pockets of time that make up my hidden hour.

➤ Have no deadlines. This means that they can sit on this list for a very long time before they become urgent.

➤ Require no referral to others. This means no one else is waiting for the tasks to be completed.

➤ Require no follow up. They sit alone, not in a sequence of events. Again, this means that there is no danger that someone is waiting for completion.

➤ Require no energy. I need to be able to knock one of these off when my energy is low.

➤ Require no brain. I don't want to do these when I am at my best. I want to do them when I feel like one of the living dead!

One hour per day equals around 20 hours per month. If I offered you a free assistant who would come in for half a week at the end of every month to make sure all of your little, easy, simple tasks were accomplished, I'm sure that you'd agree like lightning! But that is exactly what the hidden hour is – a free resource; an opportunity to get these tasks off your list, without really investing any *extra* time in them. The time flows anyway. Your decision is whether to stand still while the kettle boils, or bang off that e-mail. Once this becomes a habit, it can have an enormous impact on your productivity.

Break up large tasks into smaller ones: the sliced loaf technique

Remember the Apollo Moon Programme? Some things are simply too large to be accomplished in one fell swoop. Lots of things on our to-do list will simply be too large to accomplish in a day. It makes sense to break these up into the smaller constituent parts, and then programme these into your schedule. Imagine slicing a loaf. You start off with a single item – the loaf, but end up with lots of smaller pieces – the individual slices. For example, perhaps you are tasked with producing the next annual report for your organisation. In fact, this is really a series of smaller tasks, including:

➤ write the copy
➤ organise photography
➤ create a design brief
➤ select and meet with a designer
➤ prepare the database for mailing
➤ proof the draft
➤ find a printer and negotiate a price
➤ stuff the envelopes and post them.

Every one of the above is a 'slice' of the overall task, which can be placed on a daily to-do list, prioritised in order of urgency, importance and goal pay-off, and scheduled into a busy day.

If you slice your loaf early enough, and deal with the slices over a longish time period, the day of looming deadlines and mounting stress could be gone forever!

Use the switch technique

The switch technique works to question whether you are getting the most out of any period of time in your day. It works in three steps:

1 Regularly ask 'what do I intend to do with the next hour? Your answer might be 'to attend the Partnership Liaison Group', 'write up the minutes of the staff meeting', 'work on the quality standards manual' or whatever.

2 Immediately follow this question with 'Is there any other way I could use the hour more productively, in terms of achieving my goals, or helping me meet the most important challenges facing me. You might answer, 'yes – work on the Community Fund bid' – or 'take some quiet time to think through a personnel issue'.

3 If the answer is 'yes', then *switch* your priority and do the most important thing instead.

This sounds obvious. It is – it's common sense. The challenge is that we tend to get involved in the whirl of a busy day and we forget to ask these fundamental questions. Getting into the *habit* of asking them, and then acting appropriately in line with your answers, is the key.

Summary:
structure your day for maximum effectiveness

To make use of the material in this chapter you will probably need to take the following steps.

1 Identify a suitable planner. They come in all shapes and sizes, from the pocket diary to software programmes for your PC or handheld computer. There are no hard and fast rules other than to get one with which you are comfortable. I prefer those that have a daily plan, a weekly plan and a monthly plan, and have enough space to allow me to take notes, keep a journal, write down my goals, store telephone numbers etc. All of the leading brands such as Time Management International, Filofax or Day Timer do these things.

2 Commit to using a single, streamlined and prioritised daily to-do list.

3 Keep your to-do list and schedule on the same page.

4 Accept that a completely full schedule is bound to end in frustration, as interruptions and delays inevitably mean you miss deadlines and go home with lots 'still to do'. Think like a popcorn chef and give yourself a chance of success by only scheduling tasks into half of your available time.

5 Look for ways to kill two birds with one stone, and multi-achieve.

6 Put your most complex tasks into your high energy windows.

7 Put your easy 'C' tasks into the hidden hour.

8 Use the sliced loaf technique to create a number of smaller manageable tasks from one large, unwieldy one, and schedule these in over a realistic period.

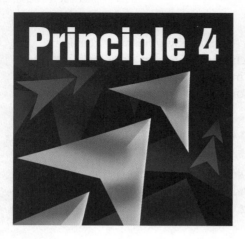

Principle 4 Protect ...

... yourself from the time stealers

Overview

By the end of this chapter you will be able to:

➤ say 'no' to tasks that you shouldn't really have to do, *without* upsetting the colleagues who make the request

➤ significantly reduce the amount of time you spend in meetings, without any loss of effectiveness

➤ remain in control of your day, even if you work in an environment filled with distractions and interruptions.

What is time stealing?

> *Part of our time is stolen from us, or else we are cheated out of it.*
>
> Seneca

So far we've examined how to be clear about what we want to achieve, and how to prioritise and organise our lives in order to succeed. Wouldn't it be wonderful if that was all we had to do – decide what we wanted and then produce schedules to give us the control we need to hit our goals?

The reality of course is rather different. Real life impacts in a variety of ways to 'steal' our precious time from us. Some of the time stealers to which Seneca was referring are self generated – they spring from our own behaviour. Others are created by the actions of other people or the cultures and working practices of our organisations. Whatever the cause, we need to defend ourselves against these time stealers if we are to protect the plans we've made.

This chapter is about protecting yourself against the time stealers. Specifically I'd like to focus on three of the most common challenges to our 'best laid plans':

➤ an inability to say 'no'

➤ spending time in meetings

➤ dealing with interruptions.

An inability to say 'no'

The earlier chapters in this book were about identifying what you want and being clear about where you need to prioritise and focus to get it. But if you can't say 'no' to others, you may find that your plans come undone. Only you can see the overview. Only you know whether tasks drive forward your goals or are critical for your work. Only you can apply these criteria, and say 'no' to tasks, activities, commitments and relationships that lie outside your boundaries.

The benefits of saying 'no' are fairly obvious:

➤ It prevents the build up of additional commitments and stops extra tasks muscling in on a packed schedule.

➤ It can create space in which to concentrate on your most important goals, or nurture yourself or engage in enhancement activities such as planning, thinking or relationship building.

In fact, without the ability to say 'no' clearly and firmly, it is very hard to avoid taking on tasks (against your better judgement) which you know will simply take an already full schedule beyond breaking point.

So why is it so hard to say the 'N' word?

Why we can't say 'no'

I don't know the key to success, but the key to failure is trying to please everybody.

Bill Cosby

There are many reasons:

➤ You may feel guilty at declining. You like to think that you're 'there' for people when they need you. In this case you need to ask yourself the following questions 'is this a one-off request, or does this person take advantage of my goodwill?'; and 'does everyone in the office turn to me for support rather than other more appropriate colleagues?'; 'is this because I'm a soft touch?'

➤ You may be unsure whether it is appropriate for you to undertake the task or not. This is particularly difficult if it is a boss or line manager asking you to do something.

> ➤ You may not want to damage a relationship. But if you are being asked to undertake inappropriate tasks regularly, perhaps this is a relationship which needs some redefining! Also consider, if you are overburdened, whether this might adversely affect a range of other relationships – with your partner, the people you manage, your team members?

> ➤ You may have to undo years of programming during which time you have learnt to say 'yes' in order not to disappoint others, or perhaps to be better liked (don't feel bad about that – we all want to be liked!). In order to learn a new behaviour, you may have to 'unlearn' an old one – and that's always a bit trickier.

How to say 'no'

The good news is that if you apply some of the lessons outlined in the earlier chapters of this book, you may find that 'no' is starting to come more easily. If you are already creating prioritised lists of tasks, if you're consistently clear about the difference between urgent and important tasks, then I'm sure that you are already declining irrelevant meetings, or turning down new commitments that do not fit with your goals or priorities. And that's great, because saying 'no' is just a habit that we can get into by practising!

Let me suggest a five-step programme:

1 Identify

You know the people who most often tend to ask for inappropriate amounts of your time. You know the circumstances in which it tends to happen. Be clear about who or what the problem is.

2 Practise

Saying 'no' is a skill. We have to practise it to become accomplished. That means getting to the point where we can refuse someone's request for our time in a polite and considerate way, rather than appearing uncaring or rude. Prepare appropriate responses, and practise using them as soon as the occasion arises. For example, if your boss gives you another 'urgent' project, ask him or her to help you prioritise by deselecting something from your current 'A' list. 'I'd love to go to the conference and report back to you. Can you choose for me whether I should delay the budget or the funding bid?' Explain the position you are being put in and suggest alternative ways forward. 'I'm happy to evaluate the outreach project for you. It will take half a day. I'm also happy to put together a training programme for the trustees – that will also take half a day. It's lunchtime so I can't do both today. Which is most important? Can someone else take one of these on board? Or can one wait?' If a colleague or someone from a partner organisation asks for your input to a project, 'It sounds really exciting and I'm flattered you think I can make a contribution; but if I take anything else on at the moment my current work will suffer. Thanks again, but no thanks'.

3 Say it quickly

Then stop. You don't have to justify yourself or make long excuses. If you get into a debate about the whys and wherefores you'll find yourself changing that 'no' to 'OK then'!

4 Stay neutral

Always use a neutral tone of voice. Try not to sound harassed or annoyed. Remember that you are in control.

5 Be strong

Some will insist. Don't get drawn into long arguments. Eventually you are bound to encounter someone who is more verbally adept and will outmanoeuvre you. Try using the 'stuck record' technique instead. Just keep smiling and repeating 'I'm sorry but I can't', 'no thanks' or 'no'.

Say 'no' to something else!

In conclusion, when you are asked to do something new, remember that your time is full. Time will not expand to fit in the new activity. So ask 'what can I drop to create space for this new commitment or activity?' 'This new project is central to my goals – which of my current tasks brings less value?' If you can identify something then you may end up saying 'no', not to the new commitment, but to the old one! If you can't identify anything, then you have a rationale, and the moral authority to feel OK about declining the new request.

Now spend some time to identify the main people who you need to say 'no' to, the circumstances or specific issues around which the problems arise and what strategy you can adopt to do this effectively and without damaging relationships.

Who do you need to say 'no' to?	What is your strategy?

Managing meetings

Some of my staff see attending meetings as a perfectly valid alternative to working.

Director of a large charity based in the south of England

For most managers, and many others working in the not-for-profit sector, meetings form a significant drain on your time reserves. Many meetings are essential. If you are a line manager, you must meet with and supervise your team. If you are a fundraiser, you must meet with potential prospects. If you work with volunteers meetings can be a valuable management tool. In fact meetings are so important, that something of a 'meetings culture' has developed in many organisations across the sector. This is dangerous because meetings can be seen as an end in themselves. They are not, they are merely a means to an end. A meeting is an input. It can only be justified if the outcome is purposeful and useful. The key question when faced with a meeting is 'is this the best use of my time, or would I get better results by spending my time in other ways?'

Do you perform effectively in meetings?

Complete the exercise opposite to gauge your relative effectiveness in the meetings you attend. Tick which box best describes your behaviours.

Common problems with meetings

Of course some meetings are essential, and it is important that they are managed well to get the most from them. I often ask people on my courses 'what problems do you encounter in meetings?' I've had almost identical answers in Budapest, Brussels and Birmingham, so I think it's fair to say that meetings produce a certain type of predictable behaviour, wherever you are! Most common complaints seem to be about those meetings that:

> have no clear purpose;

> drift off the subject;

> are dominated by one individual or group;

> are too long;

> result in arguments rather than discussion;

> are poorly attended;

> are not enjoyed by the participants;

> allow unhelpful behaviour by participants to go unchecked.

This last needs further clarification. I would classify all of the following as unhelpful behaviours (there are of course, many more than this):

> talking only about yourself and your needs;

> setting up side conversations in parallel with the main debate;

Do you perform effectively in meetings?

	Never	Sometimes	Often	Always
I decide on clear objectives before attending a meeting	☐	☐	☐	☐
I prepare thoroughly for the meetings I attend, always reading relevant papers	☐	☐	☐	☐
I listen carefully to what other participants are saying	☐	☐	☐	☐
I weigh my words before speaking	☐	☐	☐	☐
I am able to admit to being wrong	☐	☐	☐	☐
I spend time thinking about the other participants their views and what they may want from the meeting, before the meeting begins	☐	☐	☐	☐
I allow other people to finish speaking before beginning to speak myself	☐	☐	☐	☐
In more formal settings, I only address my comments through the chair	☐	☐	☐	☐
I am concerned that everyone's views should be heard	☐	☐	☐	☐
I adhere to any decisions that are made	☐	☐	☐	☐

For every time you ticked 'Never' score one point; for each 'Sometimes' score two; for 'Often' score three and for every 'Always' score four points. Then add them up.

10–20: You need to brush up in a number of areas if you are to get the most out of the time you spend in meetings.

21–30: You perform pretty well in meetings, but could still improve in some areas.

31–40: Well done. You are an exemplar of good practice. Keep it up and the time you spend in meetings will always give the pay-off you are aiming for.

> ➤ using sarcasm, smirking or poking fun at another's expense;
> ➤ being confrontational or aggressive, arguing to win at all costs;
> ➤ speaking in order to hear your own voice;
> ➤ interrupting people before they have fully explained what they mean.

In fact it is relatively easy to eliminate all of these problems, by using a few simple rules. You don't even have to use all of them. But I have spoken to hundreds of individuals over the past 10 years who have used some or all of these with a great deal of success.

Begin by asking 'why do we need this meeting?'

This question will lead you to think about the purpose of the meeting and your objectives. Meetings can have many purposes. There are briefing meetings, decision making meetings, idea generating meetings and so on. Clearly, everyone present needs to understand what sort of meeting it is. A meeting without objectives starts in a fog and continues blindly. Spending some time beforehand to work out your own objectives will mean that you are much more likely to achieve them. If you haven't got any clear objectives, then don't go to the meeting!

Ask yourself the following questions. Is the meeting really necessary? What is its purpose? Are the objectives clear? How does it help me with my goals (whether personal or professional, yours alone or those of your organisation, department or team)? If the purpose of the meeting is clear and the desired outcomes considered in advance, then the chances of successfully achieving those outcomes are significantly multiplied.

Then ask 'will the outcomes be worth it?'

An excellent way of identifying whether a meeting is delivering value for money is to work out how much it is costing. You may be surprised to know that if a director of a charity on a salary of £25,000 per year meets with three senior managers on £20,000 each, for half a day, the cost of that meeting in wages alone is almost £180. And that is without calculating any overheads! So the director should expect the meeting to bring £180-worth of results. Meetings can also be costly in less direct ways. If the outcomes of meetings are of little value, those meetings hinder the effectiveness of an organisation and its ability to fulfil its mission.

If you consistently ask these questions – 'what is the objective of the meeting?', 'do we really need it?', 'will it deliver value for money?' – you are almost sure to find that you cannot really justify at least some of the meetings that you attend. So once again, don't go!

Have a timed agenda

There should be no such thing as a 'two o'clock meeting'. There should only be a 'two o'clock to three o'clock meeting'. Your schedule won't be effective if your meetings have no time limits. Open-ended meetings are almost guaranteed to overrun. And from that moment on you will be racing to catch up. If this happens more than once then you will find that your carefully planned day will unravel and you will become increasingly fraught, keeping other people waiting for appointments as the day progresses.

However, if you make clear at the start that the meeting will end at three (or if it doesn't, it must continue without you) all of this stress can be avoided. To make a timed meeting work you must:

➤ **Agree all of the agenda items in advance** – you can't be surprised by last-minute additions, but if you have to allow an additional item, make sure it does not add to the overall time of the meeting by adjusting the amount of time down per item accordingly. So for example, if you believe that a one-hour meeting has four agenda items, allow 15 minutes each. If an additional item is added, allow only 12 minutes each.

➤ **Apportion a specific amount of time for each agenda item** – that way you can control the time you spend item by item. Many people have told me over the years that they feel that they get a better quality of focused debate if the time is limited. If time is unlimited, then there is a tendency for 'hot air' to sneak in.

➤ **Be disciplined** – try to talk only to add value to the discussion and encourage brevity among other participants.

➤ **Eliminate 'Matters arising'** – clearly you can't allow unscheduled matters arising onto the agenda, as they will throw your timing out. However, unresolved issues can be afforded the status of an agenda item proper. It simply means that if you want to add something, you either must adjust the time per item as described above, or choose to drop something from the agreed list of items to make space for your unresolved issue.

➤ **Eliminate 'Any other business'** – this is a terrible idea no matter which way you look at it. If I have something important to discuss, I don't want to introduce it at the end when everyone thinks the meeting is over, and their attention is already on the next meeting or the ride home. If it is truly important, then I'd much prefer to get their full attention. In which case it should be an agenda item in its own right. And if it isn't that important, let's have a shorter meeting!

Place a clock or watch where everyone can see it at the start of the meeting and signal to them that the meeting will end at an agreed time.

Summarise regularly

Make sure that everyone understands what has been agreed.

Agree action points

These should reflect the purpose and objectives of the meeting.

Think about the environment

Much can be achieved by a careful consideration of how the room is laid out. For example, if you want people to attend closely, don't give them deep sofas to sit on, with the heating full on and the windows closed. This sounds obvious, but how many meetings have you been in when the set up seemed carefully stage managed to send you to sleep? If you expect two people to be antagonistic towards one another, don't sit them on opposite sides of the table as this will result in lots of challenging eye contact. Rather, sit them side by side, perhaps with someone between them. If on the other hand, you feel that one person needs to make a strong appeal to another, sit those two opposite one another. Just as eye contact can be challenging, it can also be one of the most powerful tools to engender trust and understanding.

Bring positive behaviours

Just as badly managed meetings can lead to poor behaviour, I believe that it is possible to bring positive types of behaviour into meetings. Perhaps some of the most powerful are

> speaking briefly;

> supporting another speaker and encouraging others to participate;

> asking questions or seeking clarification when you don't understand;

> looking for shared positions rather than adopting rigid positions;

> talking about the group process to ensure that everyone contributes and no one is marginalised;

> listening with real attention, as opposed to waiting for people to stop speaking so you can begin again;

> asking for concrete examples to illustrate points and avoiding generalisations.

Informal meetings

Most of what we've just discussed concerns formal meetings, but much of your day may be spent in much less formal interactions with colleagues, customers or service users. These need managing too. I would argue that any discussion with a colleague, every supervision session, every phone call can benefit from a few seconds spent first thinking about:

> the purpose of the discussion and the specific objectives or outcomes you want to achieve;

> how much time it should take;

> whether this moment is a good time to have it, or can it be fitted somewhere else on your schedule.

Now spend some time to identify:

➤ any regular meetings which you could easily give up;

➤ any regular meetings which you could help to improve;

➤ any team members or colleagues with whom you could produce a 'meetings improvement' strategy.

Jot down some specific actions to take in the box below:

Actions to improve meetings:

15 meeting tips

1   If you can resolve the issue without having a meeting – cancel the meeting.

2   The fewer the people, the shorter the meeting – so keep meetings as small as possible in terms of who you invite.

3   If the purpose of the meeting is to resolve a disagreement, canvass support from likely allies for your position before the meeting, and rehearse your arguments. This can also serve to short-circuit a lot of discussion.

4   When you plan a meeting, be sure to include travel times to and from the venue on your schedule.

5   Avoid meetings when people are likely to be at their lowest ebb, such as immediately after lunch.

6   Make sure that the most important items are at the beginning of the agenda. That's when people are concentrating most.

7   Make sure that phone calls are always diverted or the answering machine is on during meetings.

8   Whenever possible, have your meeting on neutral ground. That way you are not likely to be interrupted by colleagues 'just passing', or delivering 'urgent' messages.

9   Always work out your objectives and what you need to say to whom before the meeting begins.

10   If you anticipate problems, make sure that those who need to know are briefed before the meeting begins.

11   Don't talk in order to hear the sound of your own voice. Only speak if your contribution moves the meeting forward in some way.

12   If possible, try to schedule meetings before lunch. These meetings always finish on time!

13   Always begin on time. If a key person is not there for the first agenda item, shuffle the agenda.

14   Ask the chair to give constant reminders as to how much time is left and whether the agenda is on track to finish at the prescribed time.

15   Ensure that all decisions are recorded in writing. Ask for clarification of 'what has been agreed' before this happens.

Dealing with interruptions

Interruptions can be very damaging as they result in:

> **priority inversion** – time that has been reserved for 'A' list priorities may be hijacked by less important matters.

> **broken concentration** – you may be performing at a high level of focus and concentration. The interruption breaks that. Once the 'zone' of full concentration is gone, it can be hard to get back again.

> **disrupted schedules** – these can be disrupted if the interruptions are lengthy or repeated, meaning deadlines are missed, meetings delayed etc.

Our work is interrupted usually when one of three things happen:

> when other people approach us in person while we are engaged in important work;

> when other people phone us;

> when we unsuccessfully attempt to phone other people.

It is of course unreasonable to expect that we can get through our working life without interruptions. Indeed sometimes they are an essential part of the job. But we do need to be able to manage them, to stay in control, in order to prevent the problems listed above and the attendant frustration, sense of loss of control and related stress. It stands to reason that the more unmanaged interruptions there are during the course of a day, the more disrupted that day will be. We need therefore to employ specific strategies to handle our inevitable interruptions and limit the damage as much as possible.

When others approach us in person while we are engaged in important work

There are two considerations – to make it clear that the interruption is unwelcome, but at the same time to avoid giving offence. Clearly, unless carefully handled, it will be difficult to achieve both of these contradictory outcomes.

To get around this you should use the most powerful device you possess to send clear and unequivocal messages – your body. Psychologists and anthropologists agree that when we communicate, 55% of the message is delivered by our body language. This compares to 7% for the words and 38% for the tone in which they are spoken. Try this. The next time someone approaches your desk *stand up*. Remain standing even if they sit down. You should be polite and continue to smile, but the action of standing up will send a clear signal that:

> the interruption should focus on business and under no circumstances cross that rather fuzzy line into 'chatting';

> that it should be short and to the point.

'Schedule in' your interruptions – use open consultation, not open door

I know of one manager who makes it clear to his staff that he is free to be interrupted between 4.30pm and 5.00pm, which really means 'don't interrupt me before 4.30pm'. By channelling his expectations into this 30-minute slot he is able to:

> allow his interruptions to accumulate until he is ready to deal with them;

> place his 30-minute slot at the end of the day, a period when his personal energy is low;

> ensure that other periods in the day, when he has more focus and energy, are free from interruptions. These periods he uses to schedule in 'A' priority work.

This example demonstrates the difference between an 'open *door*' policy and an 'open *consultation*' policy. Open door usually means that staff are given permission to seek a manager's attention when it suits them. The staff are in control, and the manager will suffer the frustration of constant interruption as a result. Open consultation means staff can still reach a manager to talk issues over or consult on a problem every day – but he or she remains in control of when this happens.

When people phone us

When Thomas Edison sought a patent for the electric telephone, questions were asked in Congress. It seems that the idea of an instrument which was placed inside the home and which would give immediate and shrill notice that the householder's attention was required was considered an excessive imposition by the private and retiring Victorians. His defence was remarkable in its ingenuousness and simplicity. 'You don't have to answer it'!

How wrong could he be! The telephone is a siren. It is impossible to resist. It offers the promise of excitement, interest, friendship or social engagements. It tells us that we are important and popular. Of course we *have* to answer it. If you don't believe me try a simple experiment. The next time your phone rings, sit on your hands and stare at it. See how long you can resist! And when we do succumb to the temptation and answer, of course we lose control of our carefully prepared schedule as our new interlocutor launches into 'I'd just like to run over the budget figures one more time...'

The solution is to intercept the call before it reaches us. So:

> if you have a receptionist or personal assistant, ask him or her to hold your calls if you are working on 'A' priority tasks;

> if you have an answering machine put it on;

> always re-route your calls if you are working on your golden goals, engaged in high energy window activities, or having 'a meeting with yourself'.

When we unsuccessfully attempt to phone other people

Phoning other people can suck our schedule into a black hole.

Time evaporates when:

➤ we try a number of times to ring an elusive colleague or contact. They never answer their phone or they seem always in a meeting or away from their desk;

➤ you need to speak to someone in order to move a project forward. They are not in when you call and don't return your call, leaving you in limbo;

➤ the person you ring can't answer your query and promises to ring you back;

➤ you are put on hold; and you hold ... and hold ... and hold....

There are a number of techniques which can help to deal with problems such as these and result in much more efficient phone time:

1 If the reason for the call is important try to arrange a telephone appointment with the other person to discuss it. This ensures that you will get through to them, that they will be prepared and will have any information they need at their fingertips.

2 For people you speak to fairly often (a few times a week), put together the things you talk about into a 'bundle' and try and cover them in a single, pre-scheduled call. This will mean that one scheduled item replaces many interruptions to your schedule.

3 Never rely on a call being returned. If someone is not available, ask when they will be. Then inform whoever is taking the call that you will ring back at that time and ask that they put the time in the diary of the person you are trying to speak to.

4 Schedule in high priority calls at the beginning of the day.

5 Leave low priority calls until the end of the day.

Create a plan to reduce inappropriate interruptions

Record below the specific techniques you think would reduce the number and length of the interruptions you suffer from. Think about who the main offenders are; can you reprogramme their behaviour? Identify whether there are periods of the day when you are likely to get more interruptions than otherwise. Can you create a schedule to accommodate these?

Ways to reduce interruptions

1 _____

2 _____

3 _____

4 _____

5 _____

6 _____

7 _____

8 _____

9 _____

10 _____

Summary:
protect yourself from the time stealers

1 Remember the 'unholy trinity'; the time stealers who spirit our time away without our permission:

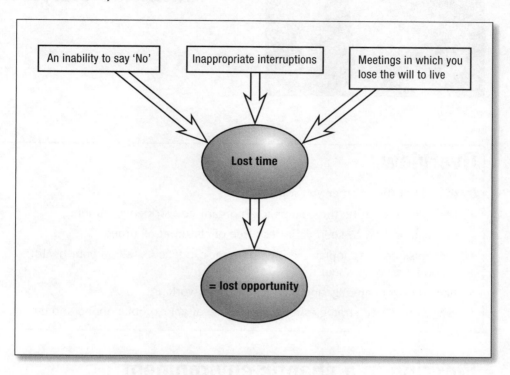

2 Use the five-step approach to saying 'no' to inappropriate requests for your time. Remember that turning such requests down enables you to focus in areas which make a real difference.

3 Never attend a meeting when it has no clear and agreed purpose. Always ask the participants in advance what the point of the meeting is. Remember that avoiding meetings which serve no purpose will free up time, which you can use to make a difference.

4 Ask, 'will the outcomes be worth the time and money that this meeting will cost?' If not, can we find an alternative way of making progress?

5 Specify and keep to an 'end time' for every meeting.

6 Try to 'channel' interruptions into predetermined periods when your energy is likely to be low. Don't take calls when working on very important tasks.

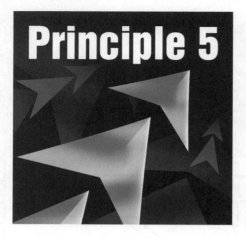

Principle 5 Organise ...

... your environment to maximise efficiency

Overview

By the end of this chapter you will:

➤ have discovered the three steps to an organised work environment

➤ understand how to keep your desk free of clutter at all times

➤ recognise how an unplanned environment can take its toll on your health – and what to do about this

➤ have thought carefully about effective home working

➤ have considered strategies for effective use of your mobile phone and e-mail.

Working in a chaotic environment

Let's face it, 'the paperless office' is a myth. Despite the information technology revolution, it now seems that there is more paper being generated than ever before. We are all affected by this paper avalanche. It has been estimated that:

➤ nearly half of everything we file is held on file somewhere else;

➤ over five billion pieces of junk mail are sent in the UK each year;

➤ the recent development of junk faxes, adds to the burden of unwanted and unnecessary paper.

And it's not just paper. Information overload comes to us in many forms, via the airwaves, the Internet and billboards to name but a few. It has been estimated that a copy of a weekday broadsheet newspaper contains more information than a contemporary of Shakespeare would have been exposed to in a lifetime!

So clearly, we are attracting more paper and information than ever before. And that would be OK if only we threw the old paper away! But for some reason, many of us find this very hard to do. The average office attracts 40% more paper every year than it throws away! Where does it all go? Inderjit's experience is all too common:

> **Case study:** 'On my desk I have three piles. The very urgent pile, which needs doing today. The quite urgent pile, which needs doing as soon as I've done the first pile. And the not urgent pile, which is everything else. As well as those, pushed to the back is a reading pile. On that goes all of my magazines, brochures, circulars and so on that I'd like to catch up on when I have a chance. The trouble with this system is that it would currently take me about a week to work through the 'must be done today' pile! No matter how hard I work, the piles keep growing. Once every couple of weeks I try to sort them out, but this just seems to take half a day and result in lots of other little piles that get spread across the desk and when that is full, across the floor.'

Does it matter if we have an untidy environment?

Yes it does! A chaotic environment like that found in many offices results in:

➤ **broken concentration** – it has been found that every piece of paper on your desk will 'catch your eye' and distract you up to five times per day;

➤ **wasted time** – my estimate is that we may spend up to 30 minutes every day shuffling through paper clutter looking for specific documents;

➤ **wasted money** – based on the above, a regional charity with a staff salary bill of £500,000 per year, will be paying out around £35,000 per year on people looking for paper on their desk!

➤ **more stress** – a chaotic environment seems to close in around us, prompting a feeling that we are out of control (which is probably true);

➤ **missed opportunity** – how many funding deadlines have been missed because the CVS bulletin which advised of a new funding programme was half way down the reading pile? How many training courses that would have solved a problem have been unattended because the brochure disappeared to the bottom of an 'in' tray, for consideration 'tomorrow'?

How to cope: three steps

In fact, the principles of managing paper more effectively are not difficult, but the benefits of applying them can be significant. There are three steps to coping effectively:

1   attract less paper;

2   have one project on your desk at any one time;

3   deal with each piece of paper immediately.

Attract less paper

If you attract less paper to you, you will have less to deal with. So try these techniques.

➤ Get off the mailing lists of periodicals you never read.

➤ If possible, ask for a verbal report or a presentation rather a written report.

➤ If a written report is absolutely necessary, ask for a summary rather than the whole thing.

➤ Ask not to be sent minutes you will never read of meetings you never attend.

➤ Don't send memos to people in the next office – walk in and tell them instead.

➤ If everyone in the organisation needs a memo, pin one copy on the notice board.

➤ Don't ever say 'leave it with me'. It's just asking for trouble! Before you know it numbers of manila files will have been left on your desk by a grateful and relieved colleague. See what we said about saying 'no' in chapter 4.

➤ Much material can be identified as junk mail before it is even opened. The company livery on the front of the envelope or the fact that they've got your name wrong is a dead giveaway! Throw this into the bin without opening it.

➤ Don't get rid of telesales people by saying 'send me some information on your training course/computers' or whatever because they will! Simply say 'no' instead.

➤ Keep all of your personal notes, plans, records of phone conversations etc. in your planner or diary, rather than scattered across the desk or filed in various places.

Have one project on your desk at any one time

You can only really focus on one project at a time. So whatever you are working on, clear your desk of all other paperwork which does not relate to that project. When you finish working on this project, file all of the related papers, leaving a clear desk for the next major task or undertaking. This one brain, one project, one desk approach means that you are much less likely to be distracted by other ideas or items competing for your attention. One manager I worked with kept her 'in tray' on a colleague's desk! (The colleague complained, so the offending tray was placed on the top of a tall filing cabinet at the other end of the office!)

Don't let paper accumulate: deal with every piece of paper you encounter immediately

Thirty years ago, time management guru Alan Lakein said, 'handle each piece of paper only once'. This advice holds true today. As you work at your desk, you will of course find that other paper is passed to you, via the mail or colleagues. To maintain your focus and prevent clutter you must deal with each one without delay and not allow them to build up. Fundamentally, there are only three choices as to how to deal with a piece of paper. These are:

➤ take action immediately

➤ file it for later

➤ get rid of it.

Take action immediately

This doesn't mean stop your work every time a new piece of paper lands on your desk. But it does mean that at the first appropriate opportunity you should deal with whatever has built up. If your work flow is interrupted by, for example, a meeting, deal with the paper that has accrued as soon as you return to your desk before getting involved in other tasks. It is all too easy to push newly arrived paper to one side for later, but if this becomes a habit, you'll soon feel like you are drowning in it. So the question to ask is 'can I do this right now, without disrupting my work flow too much?' If the answer is 'yes', do it. If not, go to the next step.

File it for later

You should delay action if:

➤ dealing with it now would interrupt you and distract you from completing more important work;

➤ the task is too big to accomplish right away;

➤ you need to consult with others or gather more information;

➤ the task is relatively unimportant;

➤ something else has to be accomplished before this can be actioned. For example, you may need to complete a business plan before applying for funds.

If you decide to delay action, you need to get the material off your desk to avoid distraction. But you also need to avoid the danger of 'out of sight, out of mind'. The solution is to make a commitment to deal with the work at a later time or date, put a note in your diary or planner to prompt action at the appropriate time and then file the paperwork out of sight.

Other filing tips include:

➤ Quickly scan newsletters, periodicals and magazines for the very few items that may be of interest to you. Cut them out and keep them in a box file specifically kept handy for the purpose. Then throw away what remains of the publication.

➤ Better still, create a tit-bits file on your hard drive for interesting ideas, thoughts, facts and information. Record your tit-bits here, then throw away the original paper.

> Keep one drawer in your desk as a low priority file. Put all of the paper relating to your 'C' tasks in this drawer (see chapter 3). During the hidden hour (see chapter 4) grab something from the draw and rattle it off. Every couple of months go through the drawer and throw away everything that has died a natural death.

> Regularly purge your filing system. If your filing system is also used to archive material, pretty soon it will become silted up, difficult to navigate and unclear to others.

Get rid of it

There are two ways to do this:

Option 1: give it to someone else

You should pass paperwork on if it is more appropriate for a colleague to deal with it. Don't pass it on if it is better to throw it away (see below) – that just gives someone else a headache. But if the paper should have gone to another person in the first place, or delegating responsibility for dealing with it is appropriate, by all means pass it on. The only rule, as with every other choice, is do it immediately.

Option 2: throw it away

Hoarding paper is a problem in all workplaces. You may think that you need all that material you have accumulated over the years. But when you took on the job, did you need your predecessor's paper? Of course not. You simply got on and did the job without all the stored backlog of information. You may even have taken a 'new broom' and thrown piles of archived material away. And when you leave the job, your successor will do exactly the same. What does this mean? It means that if you can do without your predecessor's paper, and your successor can do without your paper – you can probably do without your paper as well. So throw it out!

Of course, don't throw anything away that you need for legal reasons, anything to do with financial accountability or things that are mission critical. But these things notwithstanding, once you start to think critically about keeping paper, you will find that a large proportion of the stuff is not necessary. In fact, the discussions that I've had over the years tend to suggest that around 80% of material that is filed is never looked at again until the day that it's thrown out! (Remember the 80/20 rule? Well, here it is again.)

If you find it difficult to throw paper away, try one of the following techniques:

The specific use technique

When a piece of paper arrives on your desk, ask 'what specific future use does this paper have?' If you are not clear on this, or you find yourself thinking 'it might come in useful one day', you probably don't need it. So bin it!

The double wastebasket technique

This is a technique used in over 50 countries across the world. Simply have two wastebaskets. One is a regular wastebasket, for your sweet wrappers, dry biros and paper that is clearly rubbish. The other wastebasket should be taller. The base should be rectangular or square with enough area to accommodate a sheet of A4. Something like a kitchen swing bin without the lid is ideal. It sits next to the regular wastebasket and acts as a holding bay for papers that you think you *might* need, but you're not sure whether you'll *definitely* need.

When you get a bit of paper that fits that description simply drop it into the holding bay bin. If you need that paper again, you can find it. If, after two or three months you haven't needed it, the chances are you never will. At this point delve to the bottom of the pile, pull out those papers that are two or three months old, and without looking at them again, drop them into the regular wastebasket.

You will find that this technique saves hours of sorting through piles, making sub-piles, considering whether and how to act and generally being distracted from your real work. Remember not to put genuinely important papers into this system – keep them safe – and if you are still worried about accidentally losing something that will become important, console yourself that you can always get another copy from the sender!

Case study: The Laundry Lads is a project in the North West. Alan was a development worker working with older people on a deprived inner city estate. He had met Muriel, a 72-year-old lady who was caring for her very frail husband, Bill, in high-rise accommodation. Bill was incontinent and, though frail herself, Muriel was forced to wash piles of clothes every day. She had nowhere to hang the washing to dry, so had tried the launderette. This meant struggling up and down stairs (the lift was often broken) and taking the bus (there was no local launderette). Alan thought that a project to collect dirty laundry and then return it, washed and pressed on the same day could have a transformational effect on the quality of life of older people like Muriel and her husband.

But to set up such a project, Alan had to undertake a lot of research and development work, and this meant collecting an enormous amount of paper. Statistics regarding levels of need were furnished by the council, the names and contact details of specialists who could advise on everything from running volunteers to preparing a medical case for funding were collated; details of funders were summarised; meetings were set up to discuss the initiative. And this paper arrived in a constant, daily flow.

To deal with the data, and keep a clear desk, Alan used all of the strategies we have listed above. Whenever he was given an application form for a local charitable trust, he filed it and recorded a note in his diary to remind him to fill it in on a future date. When a meeting was set up, he recorded venue, date, time and agenda in his planner, then threw away the paper he had been sent with these details. When statistics from Age Concern arrived regarding levels of poverty among older people, he typed the pertinent ones onto his hard disk immediately and then threw away the paper. When he received details of a training course on the latest best practice in volunteering, he passed the paper on to his boss with a request that she send him on it. The result was a clear desk used to process work, rather than store it, less stress, a greater sense of control and less deadlines missed.

Now put together an action plan to manage paper and secure a clear desk. Think about specific actions you can take, procedures that could be changed, and colleagues or management with whom you may have to negotiate a behaviour change.

Action plan – managing paper

1 _____

2 _____

3 _____

4 _____

5 _____

6 _____

7 _____

8 _____

9 _____

10 _____

Ergonomics

The problem with many workplace environments is that they do not take into account our own body design. Your spine, for example has not significantly changed in its design for perhaps a million years. It was designed to facilitate movement and in certain positions is very strong. In other, 'unnatural' positions – those for which it was not designed – it becomes significantly weaker and prone to injury. Unfortunately, the posture many of us adopt when sitting at a desk and computer is just such an unnatural position. If we spend large amounts of time in the same, fixed unnatural position, it is possible to do serious, long-term and debilitating damage. Ergonomics involves studying the 'shape' of our work environment to better fit our own design, and therefore compensate for the pressure placed on our bodies by the modern office. If you spend a lot of time on desk work, then you must ensure that your workstation is set up ergonomically. A failure to do so could lead to:

> stress injury through repetitive tasks such as typing;

> back and neck injury as the musculoskeletal system is placed under long-term strain if your seat, computer screen and desk are not properly aligned;

> time lost through sick leave if the problems become acute;

> quality lost through feeling below par if the problems are long term.

The problem is growing. It has been estimated that:

> up to one third of worker time lost to illness has to do with work-related musculoskeletal pain;

> compensation claims have risen massively since the 1980s;

> a great many of these are down to poor ergonomic working environments.

What can you do about it?

Prevention is better than cure. A first step should be to visit your GP if you are concerned. You could also identify a physiotherapist who specialises in setting up workstations and seek advice here. Based on your size and frame it is sometimes possible to make small adjustments to the height of your desk and chair (relative to one another and the position of the VDU screen and keyboard). Or you could invest in an ergonomic chair, specially designed to alleviate any pressure on your spine. These are expensive on the face of it (they range from about £300 upwards) but one of these could represent a long-term saving for your organisation if it prevents the loss of a valuable staff member for a prolonged period, together with the cost of employing a temporary replacement. My view is that any organisation that is interested in the welfare of its staff should take this issue seriously.

Personal measures you can take include:

> Setting an alarm on your PC or desk every hour or so to tell you it is time to go walkabout. Even a short break of a couple of minutes will serve to ease the pressure that builds on your spine when you stay in a sitting position for any length of time.

> Taking up an exercise/recreation regime which helps with flexibility and core strength, such as pilates or yoga.

> Visiting your GP at the very first sign of pain or discomfort. You won't be able to tough this out. These problems tend to be cumulative – so the longer you go without taking action, the harder it will be to repair any damage fully.

Please remember that you must seek proper advice from a qualified person, such as your doctor or a qualified physiotherapist, before taking any action that might have repercussions on your health.

Working from home

The advantages

Working from home is a rising trend. There are a good many advantages to this way of working:

> Every week you will save hours and hours previously spent commuting.

> You are less likely to suffer interruptions from colleagues.

> You can be more flexible and creative with your time. As I write this, it's twenty minutes to nine on a Thursday evening. There was nothing on TV so I thought I'd do an hour 'on the book'. Normally this would be dreadful practice, but I know that I'll be able to take time off to compensate.

Some problems

On the other hand, there are of course disadvantages.

> It becomes harder to separate home and work life. You will find that you are more likely to get calls after hours from workaholic colleagues.

> You need discipline to stay focused. The fridge and kettle constantly beckon....

> You need discipline to break that focus and stop working when it is time. And even then, as you sit downstairs eating your evening meal, you think, 'I could just boot up again quickly and bang off that letter'. Before you know it, you've forgotten how to switch off.

> It can be lonely. If you work for a number of days without the (sometimes welcome) distractions offered by colleagues, you can feel very out of touch with the world.

> If you have small children, they are unlikely to accept readily that one minute you are in 'parent' mode, the next you are taking an important call and you have mysteriously switched to 'professional' mode. It's hard to act professionally when they are screaming in the background.

> You are less likely to have adequate space than if you work in a traditional office – and the office arrangement is less likely to be ergonomically set up.

Successful home working

With a few simple rules, working from home can be an excellent way of retaining focus, using your high energy window (see chapter 3) and delivering high quality work. These rules are:

> Break up your day. Don't spend the whole day slaving over a hot PC. You'll quickly become exhausted and, over a period of days disenchanted. Spend some time on 'A' type activities but also include some 'B' and 'C' tasks (just a few).

➤ Move physically as often as possible. Sit down to type, stand up to make calls. If you have enough space, set up sub-stations to work from.

➤ Make appointments outside of your home. If it is not too disruptive, and if it doesn't defeat the object of working from home in the first place, try and break up your day with outside meetings.

➤ Try to ensure that the room you choose for your office has good ventilation, good natural light and is in a quiet part of the house.

➤ Have a dedicated phone and fax line fitted to create distance between your home and your work time.

➤ Don't set up the office too far from the front door. It is possible to spend entire mornings sprinting between urgently demanding door bells and office phones.

➤ If your home phone rings downstairs, and you are working upstairs, ignore it – you are at work.

➤ Work regular hours. This provides a useful psychological safety net of 'getting into the habit' for you. It will also help your family respect your work time.

➤ Ban the family from the office. This provides a physical barrier for them. They can talk to you when you're 'at home'. When you're in your office, you're 'at work'. Without this barrier you'll soon begin to yearn for the relatively few and easy-to-control interruptions practised by your colleagues in the (real) office!

The mobile office – your phone and PC

I know that the current trend is towards evermore and greater connectivity. We are all supposed to be one big happy electronically wired-up family. But I'd like to challenge that. I recently read that we make more phone calls in a single day than we did in the whole of 1983. Are we so much more efficient? Or might most of the calls we receive be relatively unimportant, or even downright useless? (Sometimes I think if I hear just one more person on a train saying brightly into their mobile 'I'm just coming into the station, I can see you on the platform' I won't be responsible for my actions!) I don't think we need mobiles, most of the time at least. They're useful in emergencies, but for most purposes there are other – often more efficient – ways of doing things.

Here's what I propose. By all means carry a mobile phone. But never, ever, switch it on. Unless it's an emergency. Tell people that you don't own a phone. The result – no one will phone you. They will leave messages on your office voice mail and you will be able to deal with them in order of your priority, at a time of your choosing. Magic!

Managing e-mails

The main advantage of e-mail is that it is fast. You can send documents or messages around the world (almost) in the blink of an eye and that makes for a powerful communication tool. But like any other tool, it can be used purposefully or abused.

Some of the disadvantages associated with e-mail use are:

➤ Spamming, or junk e-mailing is on the increase. Every junk e-mail is a potential distraction.

➤ It looks like work, but it might not be. You can spend hours sorting and filing e-mails, but this 'busy-ness' delivers nothing in terms of helping you with what is important.

➤ It is addictive. How many times a day do you check your e-mail? If you check it more than three or four times you may be hooked (unless, of course you are waiting for an important communication). At the very least you could be said to be spending time in the 'neither urgent nor important' type of activity described in chapter 2.

➤ E-mail is an inefficient medium for certain types of communication, such as those that require debate of some kind, those that contain complex information or those that need the personal touch.

Strategies for effective e-mail use

➤ **Be private** – resist posting your e-mail address on the Internet through message boards or web pages. If you do, your address may end up on a spammer's list.

➤ **Be polite** – the speed at which we bang out e-mails might lead to a rather clipped summary style. Be careful that you are not coming across as curt or abrasive. Good long-term work relationships can be damaged by poor e-mail use.

➤ **Speak in person** – you may regularly exchange numerous e-mails with certain colleagues on a particular subject. If this is the case, consider a phone conversation instead. Because you can react instantly to each other's thoughts and opinions, you might solve the issue at a single pass. That means one interruption to your schedules, rather than many.

➤ **Use a one way street** – on the other hand, if you simply need a 'yes', 'no' or 'go ahead'; or your purpose is simply to pass on information which requires no response; then use e-mail.

➤ **Save your breath** – keep your e-mails brief and to the point.

➤ **Use Triage** – if you get enormous quantities of e-mail, use Triage. This is the technique of quickly scanning your messages and allocating them into customised boxes such as 'Deal with now' 'Deal with later', 'Forward to someone else' and 'Delete'. Most e-mail software will allow this.

- ➤ **Break the chain** – it almost goes without saying that if you receive any communication telling you to complete a quiz ('you must answer every question') then pass it on to 10 people, you should bin it.

- ➤ **Choose your time** – don't check your e-mails in your high energy window (see chapter 3), wait until you suffer an energy dip.

- ➤ **Don't be hijacked** – when you log on, don't react to the e-mails you receive without thinking. Use the urgent versus important criteria as described in chapter 2. Only respond to those that are important. Resist those that are urgent without being important.

Action plan

Considering what you've just read concerning ergonomics, working from home, being connected and managing e-mails, put together an action plan. How many actions or behaviour changes can you put in place to improve your effectiveness?

Improving effectiveness action plan

1 _____

2 _____

3 _____

4 _____

5 _____

6 _____

7 _____

8 _____

9 _____

10 _____

Summary:
organise your environment to maximise efficiency

1   A chaotic environment will result in wasted time, less effective working and heightened levels of stress.

2   You should attract less paper and throw more away.

3   Deal with paper immediately, or almost immediately, as it crosses your desk.

4   Take proper, qualified advice on setting up an ergonomically sound workspace.

5   If you work from home, work regular hours, choose an appropriate room for your office and make it a 'family-free area'.

6   Switch off your mobile more often.

7   Use e-mail appropriately.

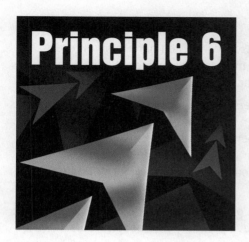

Principle 6 Take action ...

... today, not tomorrow

Overview

The message of this short chapter is that if you repeatedly take the right actions, you are almost guaranteed the results you want. So begin today.

No action = no change

If you wish to know your past life, look to your present circumstances.
If you wish to know your future life, look to your present actions.

Buddhist proverb

So far in this book you have found out about clarifying what you want to achieve, prioritising your activities to bring your goals closer and using your time and space more efficiently. But none of that will do you any good unless you follow the advice in this chapter. And it is stunning in its simplicity. Nothing will improve or change unless you take *action*. We can plan, think, ponder, reflect and learn until the cows come home – but unless it is followed up with action, nothing will change.

Why actions speak louder than words

Ninety-nine percent of success, is turning up.

Woody Allen

The ability to get things done, to start a task and see it through and to finish what one starts, can make up for limitations of intellect, character and talent. In the early days of the Soviet Union Joseph Stalin, not blessed with the oratorical gifts of Lenin or the organisational talents of Trotsky, worked hard to sit on every committee he could and thus inexorably increased his power. Whereas the others talked of the dictatorship of the proletariat, he took daily actions to create it!

This ability to take daily action, and to persevere is recognised as an important attribute in the search for success by even the most brilliant minds. Thomas Edison undertook more than 50,000 experiments to perfect the storage cell battery. He is reputed to have argued that none of the failed experiments were really failures, because each one brought him a step closer to finding the correct solution.

Whatever someone's level of intelligence or talent, perseverance and focused activity will take them a long way. You have probably met people yourself who, despite being not quite the sharpest saw in the toolbox, have done well because they are prepared to put in the work, or to act on their ideas. If you are blessed with some of those qualities that Joe Stalin lacked (intellect, character and talent) as well as a predisposition towards action – then I believe that there is very little that you cannot achieve!

Get the habit

Taking action is a habit. It is a frame of mind. The more actions you take, the more likely you are to take successful action. Get into the habit now. Go back to the passages of this book that you have already read. Consult your action plans. Find something you plan to do but haven't done yet. Put down this book, and take that action, now!

Tackle procrastination

If you are twenty years old tomorrow, you may look forward, all things being equal, to another sixty years of life. So there's plenty of time to achieve everything you want, right? Not quite. As those of you over a certain age will testify, time accelerates as you get older (Einstein missed that one). And once the time stealers have done their worst, there's less time left than you think! Procrastination is your enemy. It puts barriers in the way of you reaching your goals. But you can tackle procrastination – try some of the techniques described below.

BANJO technique

This acronym stands for **B**ang **A N**asty **J**ob **O**ff. The idea is that when you arrive at work with an unpleasant task hanging over your head, you have a simple choice. Let it lie and get on with other stuff – in which case it will gnaw at the back of your mind. Or do it first, in which case you get it done, out of the way and you enjoy the relief that this brings. If you use the BANJO method, even the most unpleasant days just get better and better as they go on.

Cold plunge

When I was a boy in Blyth, about 15 miles north of Newcastle, we used to bunk off school and go for a swim in the sea – the North Sea. Once you were in and swimming it was OK, the problem was actually getting into the icy waters. Some of my friends preferred to strip on the beach and wade in inch by inch. Personally I preferred diving off the end of the pier. Once you got over the initial shock you were fine. The same thing applies to a whole range of work challenges, from difficult conversations with colleagues to the production of the annual report. Putting it off while still worrying about it can simply serve to blow the whole thing out of proportion. Anticipation of the unpleasantness can be far worse than the real thing. So dive right in – more times than not you'll find it's not as bad as you think.

Avoid deactivation words and phrases

Deactivation words and phrases allow you to put off taking action. They include 'tomorrow', 'later', 'next week', 'when I'm ready', 'some other time'. More often than not they really mean 'never'. If it really needs doing, do it now!

Nobody's perfect

Sometimes we don't get things finished because we need more time to 'get it right'. Of course you want to do a good job – a great job, but you also have to be careful not to become too much of a perfectionist. It is possible to suffer from a kind of paralysis by analysis – too much thinking, reworking, attention to unnecessary detail – and not enough completion. Remember that the first 20% of the thinking, writing or planning you've done will get you your first 80% of success. From then on you are locked into a diminishing scale of return. It's better to complete today, and move on to the next challenge, than lose time endlessly crossing 't's and dotting 'i's.

Action plan

List overleaf things you have been putting off. Give yourself a deadline to finish them. Schedule them into your diary. If the task is too big, break it down using the 'sliced loaf' technique.

Dealing with things you put off – action plan

1 _____

2 _____

3 _____

4 _____

5 _____

Summary:
take action today, not tomorrow

1 Tomorrow never comes. The only bit of time we truly control is now. Use it.

2 If you let unpleasant issues hang over you, they will gnaw at your happiness. Take action to deal with them today.

3 Remember the words of Will Rogers: 'Even if you're on the right track, you'll get run over if you just sit there'.

Principle 7 — Nurture yourself ...

... and survive the pressure

A poor life this, if full of care,
We have not time to stop and stare

William Henry Davies

Overview

By the end of this chapter you will have learned:

➤ how to spot if you are under too much pressure

➤ the tell-tale signs of impending 'burn-out' and what to do about it

➤ how to identify where your stress comes from

➤ how to motivate yourself to take appropriate action

➤ thirteen powerful stress management techniques.

What is stress?

We tend to think of stress as primarily a psychological condition, characterised by feelings of worry, confusion, or being out of control or overwhelmed. It is generally accepted that stress can lead to poor work performance and a significant degree of unhappiness. The ability to be stressed is, however, a perfectly natural part of our make-up. In fact is it true to say that, without stress, we wouldn't be here today.

Stress is an automatic response to changes in environment, and it enabled our ancestors to stay alive in a variety of circumstances. Whether these circumstances were attacks from neighbouring tribes or the changing of the seasons signalling coming scarcity of warmth and food, those that became stressed quickly enough tended to take appropriate action. This has been called the 'flight or fight' response; a series of automatic physiological changes that prompt swift and decisive action. These changes include a rise in heart rate and blood pressure, the diversion of oxygenated blood to the parts of the body best able to deal with the danger (specifically, and most obviously, the legs, arms and upper body), an increase in the breathing rate and a release of hormones and chemicals such as adrenaline into the bloodstream. In short we are descended from those that survived because of their ability to become stressed and who therefore lived long enough to pass on their genes.

Why too much stress is bad

The flight or fight response has served our species well so far. But too much stress, particularly if produced over a long period, can be very damaging. The problem is that when faced with any challenging situation, (which in the modern workplace may include such things as a looming deadline, a tough task or a difficult relationship) our body, prompted by our subconscious mind and the very powerful genes inherited from our forebears, reacts as if those things were an approaching sabre toothed tiger or a failed harvest. We are prompted to take decisive action. And if that is not possible or appropriate, then the cocktail of chemicals in our system stops being helpful and begins to hurt us. For example, challenging work situations which make us anxious stimulate increased levels of cholesterol and make our blood thicker. This is useful in a physical fight for survival, but in the modern world, if repeated over long periods, can result in an increased risk of heart disease.

Is stress getting worse?

According to recent studies, stress is most definitely a growing problem in the not-for-profit sector. For example, researchers commissioned by the *Sunday Times* found that social workers, youth and community workers, managers and local authority officers all experienced significant increases in stress levels between 1985 and 1997.

According to Polly Ghazi and Judy Jones, writing in *The Downshifters' Guide to Happier and Simpler Living*:

> ➤ stress accounts for 90 million lost working days every year in the UK;
> ➤ stress costs the British economy £7 billion per year;
> ➤ while average working hours in Europe are falling, in the UK they are rising.

The Gulbenkian Foundation funded a charity, Parents At Work, to study this phenomenon. The report, published in the mid 1990s found that:

> ➤ most of us put in extra unpaid hours;
> ➤ many working parents state that they don't see enough of their children;
> ➤ nearly half were working over 50 hours per week.

The European Work Time Directive recently adopted in the UK is designed to change this – but I wonder, have you noticed a difference? Many people that I talk to have not.

How to spot that you may be overly stressed

There is a whole range of mental, behavioural and physical symptoms which can be at best distressing to you and others around you and at worst, damaging to health, both physical and mental. These include:

Behavioural and mental

> a shortened temper

> irrational mood swings

> procrastination

> increased consumption of alcohol, caffeine and tobacco

> increased consumption of junk food

> lack of energy

> poor memory.

Physical

Too much stress will make you grumpy, less effective and no fun to be around. But will it really affect your health? Well, in short, most certainly. Some studies have shown that rats subjected to stressful situations by researchers, such as being placed in cages next to ferrets, or given electric shocks, suffer a decrease in the effectiveness of their immune system. Production of B and T immune cells slows right down, the killer immune cells which attack tumours are less efficient and the animals produce less essential immune chemicals such as interferon. Humans respond to stress in much the same way. Studies have shown that carers who undertake the demanding task of looking after Alzheimer's sufferers are more prone to infection, and that students produce less interferon at exam time.

Why does this happen? Basically because the autonomic nervous system that links our body and brain has two sub-systems. One sub-system heats up our body's engine, ready for action, triggering the release of sugars, fats, adrenalin and cortisol into our bloodstream, and stimulating increased heart rate, rapid breathing and perspiration. The other sub-system controls the responses which cool us down when the moment of 'danger;' has passed. This cooling down is essential if the body is to maintain its equilibrium. Our health is placed at risk when one system is repeatedly stimulated, but the other is not allowed to kick in to reverse the physical effects. If we could react to our stress by taking physical action (which biologically is what we are supposed to do) then the harmful effects of the stress would be somewhat counteracted. But most of our modern-day stress is caused by arguments with our colleagues, a constantly ringing phone or traffic lights that stay on red for too long. Physical action is hardly appropriate in these situations.

Instead, we resort to anxiety-driven behaviours such as smoking, drinking too much and gorging on fast food. In the long term these can lead directly to very damaging physical conditions, including obesity, heart disease and cancer. Sometimes we need to be good to ourselves, to find ways of nurturing ourselves through the pressure.

Don't get burned

Burn-out is a condition that has long been recognised by psychologists. Burn-out typically affects hard-working, committed, dedicated people who become emotionally, psychologically or physically exhausted. You may be in danger of burn-out if you regularly demonstrate any of the following behaviours:

➤ finding it tough to say 'no' to additional tasks or extra responsibilities;

➤ seeking perfection in your work and that of others;

➤ trying to cope with intense and sustained pressure for a prolonged period;

➤ trying to juggle conflicting priorities, or balance too many commitments;

➤ offering emotional support to other highly stressed people over a long period.

The temperature test

Burn-out doesn't happen overnight. It is the result of a slow build up of pressure which grows imperceptibly, until it is too late to redress. They say that if you drop a frog in a pot of hot water it will immediately leap out, but if you place a frog in cold water and slowly apply heat, the frog will sit in the water until it is well boiled. (And no, I haven't tried it!) You can apply a kind of temperature test to the pot in which you currently sit by answering the following questions:

The temperature test

I often feel that my levels of motivation are not as great as they once were.　　Yes/No

The quality of my work has declined in recent weeks or months.　　Yes/No

I sometimes feel a growing dissatisfaction with my job or role.　　Yes/No

These days I seem tired all the time.　　Yes/No

I am taking more time off sick than I used to.　　Yes/No

I don't feel in control.　　Yes/No

I often find myself thinking negatively – used to be much more positive than this.　　Yes/No

I avoid any confrontation.　　Yes/No

Recently I have tended to disengage from any situation
or relationship which might cause more stress.　　Yes/No

> The more times you answered 'yes', the hotter the water you're in. If you answered 'yes' five or more times, you are probably in serious danger of burn-out and need to act now.

The stress survival programme

Accept that some stress is good

Stress is always present in those situations when you feel most alive – the fairground ride, the sports event, the build up to a romantic encounter. Without stress in the workplace we would find it hard to be motivated, to perform at our best, to achieve the things of which we are proud. The level of stress which helps us leap out of bed in the morning, enthusiastically engage with tasks, operate at our optimum level, is to be sought after, not shied away from. We do our best work when some stress is present. The only difference between a diamond and a lump of coal is that the diamond had a little more pressure put on it.

There is a very real relationship between stress and performance as the graph below illustrates.

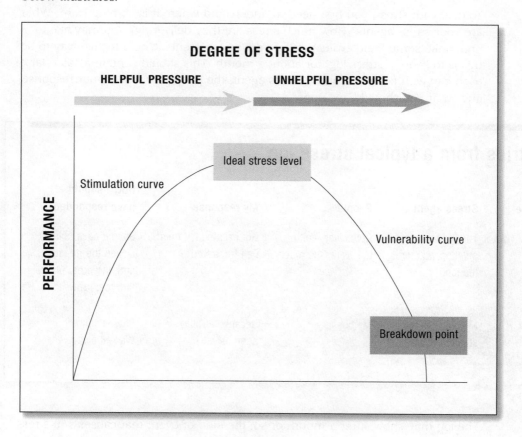

The horizontal axis equals the amount of pressure being placed by outside stress agents. The further you continue along from left to right, the greater the stress. The vertical axis represents performance levels. The graph shows how some stress is essential to stimulate us. Helpful amounts of pressure result in useful stimulation and with this our performance improves.

For each of us, there exists an *optimum* level of stress. Some people will operate best under little or no stress, whilst others need significant amounts of stress to prevent them becoming bored, uninterested and demotivated. Our ideal stress level is the point where the amount of stress and an individual's ability to cope are in balance. If more stress is added beyond this point, we enter the vulnerability curve. On this curve lie fatigue, exhaustion, mistakes, loss of confidence, ill-health and ultimately, if the stress continues to accumulate, breakdown, as the pressure exceeds our ability to cope with it.

So the first step in your stress survival programme should be to monitor the amount of stress you are under and aim to keep it close to your ideal stress level. And the way to do that is ...

Identify the stress agents

To deal with stress, you first need to understand where it is coming from. What are your stress agents? How much stress are they delivering? You may like to undertake some 'field evaluation' of your stress agents. One effective way to do this is to keep a 'stress log' for about a month. This should contain a calendar of each day with columns for the stress agent, the people involved, your response, and what you should have done.

Entries from a typical stress log

Date	Stress agent	People	My response	How I should have responded
May 14th	The management meeting was far too long	Councillor Smith talked far too much	Got irritated with him Felt frustrated	Should have politely closed the meeting and agreed to phone him tomorrow
May 15th	My boss shouted at me	My boss	Became verbally aggressive	Stayed calm Walked away

The log may show, after a month or so, the kind of event that causes you stress. It may also reveal underlying patterns that lead to the entrance of the stress agent. For example, if the first episode shown in the above log is typical, this might demonstrate that the writer does not prepare enough for his meetings, that he needs to brush up on his chairing skills, or that he needs to avoid meetings wherever possible with Councillor Smith!

As a quick litmus test you should complete the exercise below. Examine the lists of stress agents. If you regularly experience any of the following common stress agents, put a tick in the box to the right:

Work-related stress agents

Trouble with clients/customers/colleagues ☐

Having to work late ☐

A lack of job security ☐

A lack of specific skills
(e.g. managing people) ☐

Constant interruptions ☐

Deadlines and time pressures ☐

Poor systems and procedures ☐

Office bureaucracy ☐

A disorganised or chaotic working environment ☐

A workplace bully ☐

Your own attitude (e.g. a reluctance
to delegate, or an inability to say 'no') ☐

Unstimulating work ☐

Technological failure (e.g. computer crashes) ☐

Travelling to and from work ☐

Travelling associated with your job ☐

Delivering bad news to colleagues
or team members ☐

Lack of clear life/career direction ☐

Disruption of home life by
work-related demands ☐

Conflict with colleagues ☐

Too much responsibility ☐

Unable to cope with your to-do list ☐

Personal stress agents

Debt or other financial problems ☐

Illness (yours) ☐

Illness (someone close to you) ☐

Moving house ☐

Marital or partner problems ☐

Neighbour disputes ☐

Legal problems ☐

Problems with children
(school/illness/behaviour etc.) ☐

Deal with the stress

Now that you have a fair idea where the stress is coming from, you only have two options. You can *eliminate* the stress agent or find ways to *build your resistance* to it.

Finding practical strategies to do one or the other of these is what the rest of this chapter is about.

Eliminating the stress agents

I think it makes sense to approach this quite systematically in three key steps.

Step 1: target key stress agents

The first stage is to list those things that you feel you could walk away from. Are there any tasks that you can delegate? Situations you can avoid? Relationships you can change? Think first about your biggest stress agents as recorded above, but also bear in mind that, because stress is cumulative, any change for the better, to any of the stress agents you have identified, will be beneficial. Bear in mind also that it is often our own attitude that leads us to feel stressed. We create our own stress by undertaking urgent but not important tasks, refusing to delegate (or doing it badly), neglecting to seek help from others, taking on too much because we perceive that to do otherwise would let others down. It is quite possible that you are the biggest single cause of stress in your life!

Stress agents I would like to eliminate:

_____

_____

_____

_____

_____

_____

_____

_____

Step 2: decide on action

Now think about the action that you must take to eliminate the stress agent. It may be that you have to change your own behaviour. If your time management skills are the problem you will need to seek training; if you are in debt, you may have to seriously re-evaluate your spending habits and lifestyle; if you cannot say 'no' to extra work, you may have to learn how to use that word! Or it may be that you have to face up to someone else's behaviour. Perhaps a team member is consistently late, or a colleague regularly misses deadlines, or your line manager makes unreasonable or unstructured demands. Dealing with problems caused by your own or others' behaviour will, in the immediate term, have the effect of *increasing* the stress you feel. But be brave. If the action you take eliminates the cause of the stress, you will reap enormous long-term benefits.

Actions to eliminate key stress agents:

_____

_____

_____

_____

_____

_____

_____

Step 3: get motivated

Sometimes the action you need to take to remove a stress agent is relatively straightforward and simple. If so you may be able simply to focus on the problem and sort out what needs to be done. That's great. On the other hand you may have known for some time what needs to be done, but steered clear of taking the action because of the stress it will cause. If that is the case, you may need some help to get motivated.

There is an old saying that there are two types of lion tamer. One is motivated by a desire to be applauded by the crowd, the other by a desire not to be eaten. The first is motivated towards pleasure and reward; the second away from pain and negative consequences. Which are you?

Ask yourself the following questions:

What will be the negative consequences of continued inaction?

If nothing changes how will you feel in a week or another month? What will happen if the worry doesn't go away? Are you the only one who is affected by this, or are others close to you also affected? What will be the damaging consequences for them? Try to sum up these and similar issues in the box below.

What will be the positive consequences of taking action?

What will be the gains once the stress agent (or stress agents) have been eliminated? How will you feel? How will those around you feel?

Now are you motivated to grasp the nettle?

Step 4: take action

It's true that some of the actions you've identified above should be weighed and considered carefully, for they will have consequences. It's also true however that the longer you delay, the easier it will become to shy away from decisive action. Perhaps the only thing you know for sure is that if you do not take action, take control, and do what needs to be done, the stress will remain. As someone once said 'if you always do what you've always done, you'll always get what you've always got'.

Develop your resistance to stress

Removing stress agents is good. But it's not always possible. Whatever your role, teacher, parent, fundraiser or whatever, sometimes stress just comes with the territory. And if that is the case, you will need strategies to counter the stress. You will need to take the actions that will buoy you up, make you stronger, help you to recover and replenish your inner resources.

Countering strategies can be psychological or physical. They might include:

Mellowing out

> *One of the symptoms of an approaching nervous breakdown is the belief that one's work is terribly important and that to take a holiday would bring all kinds of disaster.*

> Bertrand Russell

Switching off is a habit. If you have spent the last few years focusing strongly on work and the demands of your career, if your life is very pressurised, you may need to relearn, or at least remember, how to ease off. One way of doing this is to pick up calm habits. Try consciously to do things more slowly. Drive more slowly. Eat more slowly. Talk more slowly. After around three weeks you will have begun to change permanently into a slower pitch of life!

Treat yourself more often. Take a massage, take time out to smell the roses, take a walk in the hills or on a long empty beach. How long is it since you 'got away from it all'? Even a few hours can make all the difference. Relaxation, charging up the batteries, is an essential part of nurturing yourself for the challenges ahead. It may not be urgent (there is always something more *urgent*, a meeting, a report, a decision) but it is so, so *important*.

Taking regular breathers

Every now and then go away, have a little relaxation, for when you come back to your work your judgment will be surer. Go some distance away because then the work appears smaller and more of it can be taken in at a glance and a lack of harmony and proportion is more readily seen.

Leonardo Da Vinci

The US military discovered during the Korean war that soldiers who were given regular, short breaks during route marches reached their objective before those that tried to complete the journey in one, sustained leg. Regular breaks can vastly increase your ability to cope with pressure and improve your ability to get things done. Keeping yourself under pressure for prolonged periods is counter productive. In the long run, this doesn't do you, or your organisation any favours at all. You are no good to your employer if you become ill and take time off, or if you continue to work with a short temper, impaired judgement, a negative attitude or any of the other less-than-helpful symptoms of too much pressure.

So take your holidays, keep your weekends free, only work in the evenings if absolutely essential and always take time off in lieu. Yes, this may cause you problems in the short term, but the long-term benefits to the quality of both your work and your life will be immeasurable.

Don't worry, be happy

I'm an old man and I've had many troubles, most of which never happened.

Mark Twain

Think how much time people spend worrying, about their overdraft, their children, their deadlines, the state of the nation, or what their boss or the neighbours will think.

Now consider, how much of what we worry about really matters. In fact, very little. But every worry has increased the stress we are under. I once heard of an inscription on a gravestone. It read: 'I used to worry such a lot. Now I'm dead – I've stopped'. It's probably apocryphal, but I like the sentiment. There is a very strong case for being a little more fatalistic about life. Sometimes bad things happen. If they do, we will have to deal with them; but until they do, there is little to be gained by worrying.

Life's a joke!

There is also a considerable body of opinion that suggests that laughter can have very positive benign effects on our physical and mental well-being. In the US there is even a medical magazine, the *Journal of Nursing Jocularity*, which examines the benefits of laughter and how to stimulate it. Broadly, the idea is that laughter reduces the amount of the stress hormone cortisol and stimulates the production of infection-fighting lymphocytes in the bloodstream. It lowers heart rate and blood pressure, and makes us less aggressive and hostile (prolonged feelings of hostility can be the result of stress and can contribute to heart disease). Some researchers believe that laughing increases the amount of immunoglobin in the saliva, which in turn forms a first barrier of defence against viral infections.

But even without any of the direct positive health benefits, laughter is something we all need more of. Children laugh, smile or chuckle around 400 times per day. Adults do it 15 times per day! Think how you have felt after a serious gut-wrenching session of guffawing. Not just a little chuckle or a couple of giggles, but a heavy-duty, sustained fit of belly laughing. It feels wonderful doesn't it? In terms of stress management there is a strong argument to go out now and buy a video of your favourite comedy sketches, take a trip to a comedy club or organise an evening in with close friends playing games like charades or Pictionary. Group games such as these help us lose our inhibitions, act a little more like children, stop taking life so seriously and laugh a little.

Stay healthy

If your body is in decent shape, your ability to cope with stress will be improved. We don't need to aim to become athletes, but there are practical ways to stay in shape.

➤ Cut down on foods that diminish your ability to deal with stress, such as alcohol, caffeine, saturated fats etc.

➤ Walk or cycle, rather than using motorised transport, whenever you can.

➤ Use the stairs instead of the escalator or lift.

➤ Go dancing.

➤ Do the housework twice as fast as usual. You'll find that power-hoovering can be almost as energetic as a trip to the gym!

➤ Join a gym.

➤ Buy a dog and walk it everyday.

➤ Take the kids swimming.

➤ Sign up with a charity like the British Trust for Conservation Volunteers and get stuck into some dry stone walling, ditch digging or tree planting.

Don't forget to check with a doctor if you are overweight or haven't exercised for a long time, or indeed before attempting any new exercise regime. Don't try and do too much too soon. The best exercise is regular and undertaken as part of a lifestyle choice, rather than a 'crash' attempt to quickly lose weight or deal with a stressful situation.

You could also sample some of the wide range of less conventional therapies, practices and treatments now available. Yoga, meditation, acupuncture, reflexology, aromatherapy, flotation therapy, massage can all have calming, and in some cases healing, effects. There is a massive body of evidence suggesting that taking part in some of these 'alternative' practices, together with a firm belief that they work, can significantly improve the workings of the immune system. Make sure that any practitioner you consult holds a recognised qualification and is a member of a credible and recognised regulatory body. Check these out with your GP.

Taken individually, each of the above represents a small change in habit. Taken together they could have an enormous, positive effect.

Learn to breath properly

One of the physical manifestations of too much stress is a tendency to experience shallow or irregular breathing. When this happens, the brain can be deprived of oxygen and as a result, start to misfire.

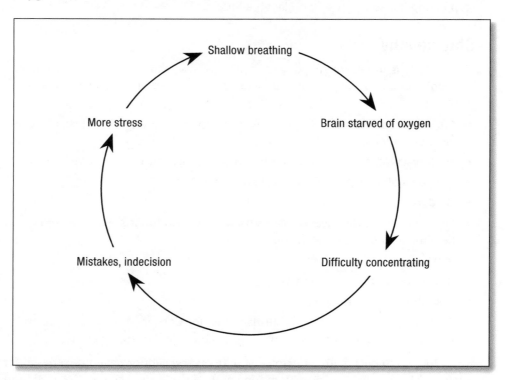

The result is difficulty in concentrating, leading to mistakes, indecision, and a generally depressed (and depressing!) performance.

When you feel stressed try a simple breathing exercise. Simply close your eyes, and take a deep breath five times. Hold each breath for a couple of seconds, before slowly exhaling through your mouth.

Sleep on it

We all need sleep, and the amount varies from individual to individual. What is important is that you get the right amount for you. And what is certain is that if your lifestyle leads to sleep deprivation, either as a result of burning the candle at both ends, or lying awake at night worrying – you will probably be less able to deal with stressful situations during the day. If you do have difficulty sleeping, try some of the following techniques:

> ➤ take more exercise;
> ➤ don't go to bed with a full stomach – eat a couple of hours beforehand;
> ➤ avoid stimulants such as tea or coffee not just before bed, but all day. Try the decaffeinated versions of these and other drinks;
> ➤ take a warm bath or shower just before bed.

Visit the well

The village well was once the place where people would come together to meet, pass the time of day, and chat with strangers. In this high pressure world, how much time do we have for people we don't already know. We push past people on the street or the tube platform, sit in our cars, sealed from the outside world. In doing so we cut ourselves off from the vast bulk of humanity and spend our lives living 'in our heads'. So try passing the time of day with people you meet. Smile at shop keepers as they give you your change. Visit the well every so often and reconnect with humanity.

Try anything once

As children we learn so greedily. Children are like sponges; they absorb facts, languages, opinions, feelings, prejudices and beliefs easily. As we get older this runaway train of learning begins to slow, and for some of us, at some point in our adult lives, it grinds to a halt. Sigmund Freud was distressed by the contrast between what he called the 'radiant curiosity of the child and the feeble mentality of the adult'. It is so easy to get into a rut – to think and feel that today will be just like yesterday; tomorrow like today. But this is so easy to change.

All we have to do is rediscover our love of learning about life – experiencing new things, taking risks, attempting things outside your comfort zone. I heard a few years back that David Bowie tries to take on board a new skill every year. I think that when I came across the article he had mastered rollerblading and was moving on to learn to speak Italian. What a fantastic idea! Choose a new, achievable, interesting and enjoyable goal each year, and spend the rest of your life being stimulated rather than bored! It will take your mind off your problems, provide a wider perspective and increase your capacity to deal with stress.

Eat chocolate!

I've read that certain chemicals in chocolate assist in the production of endorphins, which act positively to stimulate the pleasure centres of the brain. It's dirty work but someone has to do it!

Compartmentalise

Stress is cumulative, and a number of relatively innocuous stress agents, in sequence, can lead to an explosion at the end.

> **Case study:** Margaret leaves the house at 8.00am. She is quietly fuming at her partner Josh because, despite repeated promises, he has left the house with the bed unmade, yesterday's dirty clothes still on the bedroom floor, wet bathroom towels all over the landing and his breakfast dishes most decidedly not in the dishwasher. ('We both work, why do I have to do all of the tidying every morning?') She slams the car door, tries the ignition – and it won't start. However, Margaret is able to run to the corner and (just) catch the 8.05am bus which should get her to work on time. By 8.32am she's stuck in traffic, and getting later by the minute. Her mind jumps back and forth between being annoyed with Josh and worrying about being late. By the time she gets to work (at 9.20am) she is angry and frustrated. At 9.25am Paul puts his head around the door and jauntily informs her that he hasn't been able to complete the budget figures, because he had to watch Newcastle United thrash Manchester United on TV last night. With a resounding expletive Margaret storms out of the room, much to her colleague's bemusement...

One strategy to prevent this build up of negative emotion is to 'compartmentalise' each episode. Put the argument with Josh in a mental 'box'. It can be dealt with later. Put the car's failing ignition in another, you can't fix it at work, and you couldn't prevent it from happening. Put the inadequacies of public transport in another box, you can vote differently next time. This technique demands a little practice. It is related quite closely to the next technique.

Move from 'type A' to 'type B' behaviour

In the 1960s two cardiologists, Meyer Friedman and Ray Rosen, concluded that heart disease was linked to a certain type of personality. They concluded that individuals who were very driven, action oriented, ambitious and assertive were more likely to suffer from heart disease in later life. They called these 'type A' people. Type A people are more likely to take on more than they can cope with, to try to multi-task, to do things quickly and may find it difficult to delegate. They are more likely to be impatient and to be prone to worry. They may involve themselves deeply in urgent, rather than important tasks.

Friedman and Rosen also identified what they called 'type B' personalities. These appear almost the exact opposite of type As. Relatively relaxed, laid back and unhurried, type B people tend to approach problems more calmly, slowly and are not so driven by urgency and deadlines.

Very rarely does someone exclusively demonstrate type A or type B behaviour. Rather, we show tendencies towards one or the other. The challenge comes with excessive type A behaviour, because this can be linked quite clearly to excessive levels of stress. There is therefore a powerful argument to try to:

➤ determine whether you are exhibiting too much type A behaviour, and if so

➤ make a conscious effort to introduce more type B behaviour.

This means trying to be more philosophical, counting to 10, taking on fewer commitments and relaxing more. It may mean trying consciously to do things at a slower pitch, to change your over-riding mindset from one driven by 'this needs doing because it is urgent' to 'this is urgent, but it's not the end of the world if I don't do it'.

This may seem heretical to anyone who has been brought up in a western 'up and at them' culture and associates success with punch and vitality. Many of our senior politicians and business leaders have succeeded by being action oriented and aggressive. Indeed it would be hard to run a multinational conglomerate or a country without having a fair sprinkling of type A characteristics. But most of us have different challenges. Many of us believe in work/life balance and quality of life. My argument is that excessive type A behaviour may, over time, work against any attempt to bring balance to your life. I also believe that the Pareto Principle means that we get a diminishing scale of returns from the time and energy we apply, and that it is possible to achieve more by backing off and replenishing sometimes, rather than going hell for leather without respite.

Are you type A or type B?

Fill in the worksheet below. Put a tick in each appropriate box.

Type A/type B personalities

	Very often	Sometimes	Rarely	Never
You are often in a hurry	☐	☐	☐	☐
You walk fast	☐	☐	☐	☐
You talk fast	☐	☐	☐	☐
You eat quickly	☐	☐	☐	☐
You are impatient	☐	☐	☐	☐
You multi-task	☐	☐	☐	☐
You are competitive	☐	☐	☐	☐
You finish other people's sentences for them	☐	☐	☐	☐
You are ambitious	☐	☐	☐	☐
You can be critical of others	☐	☐	☐	☐
You blame others when things go wrong	☐	☐	☐	☐

Bear in mind that the following scoring and analysis is not scientific – but it *is* a useful way of giving you a pointer as to whether you need to take action.

Give yourself a score of three points for every tick in the left-hand column, two in the central left column, one in the central right column and zero in the far right column. The maximum possible score is 33, the minimum is 0.

If you score 25 or more, you exhibit a very strong type A personality. You may therefore need to take action *now* to prevent the risk of serious illness at some point in the future.

If you score between 16 and 24, you have a reasonably high tendency towards type A behaviour and should take action – not just to safeguard your health but also for the sake of those who have to live and work with you!

For scores less than 16 – the lower the score, the more your natural tendency is towards type B behaviour.

Use imagined hindsight

This is a technique advocated by Charles McCoy Jr to enhance creative thinking, in his book *Why Didn't I Think Of That?* You could use it to help you put your stress survival programme together. Simply think one year into the future. Picture yourself as being completely stress free. What does that look and feel like? How will your circumstances or behaviours have changed? What will be different about your life? Be as specific as possible. Try that now. In the box below describe how your life will look if it is relatively stress free in 12 months' time. Paint a picture of your future situation and how you will feel.

You have here a summary of the outcomes you require. Now 're-engineer' your life back to the present. Ask 'what have I done in the last year to remove the stress or build my resistance to it?' You may come up with a list like:

➤ I have delegated effectively.

➤ I prioritise well now and ignore those things that don't matter.

➤ I have cut out all of the unnecessary meetings in my life.

➤ I have lunch once a month with a close friend.

➤ I do something special with a loved one every fourth weekend.

Now try your own list.

What have I done to remove stress?

1 _____

2 _____

3 _____

4 _____

5 _____

6 _____

7 _____

8 _____

9 _____

10 _____

The next step is simple. Start *today*, to implement your list!

Finally: be your own angel

In chapter 1 we talked about the importance of being clear about the roles that you play in life. One role that you might like to take on is that of 'guardian angel watching over myself'. How can you be an angel? Look at it this way. You have to stay well, focused and happy if you are to perform your myriad roles to the very best of your ability and achieve the ambitious goals you have set for yourself. And responsibility for nurturing your strength, vitality, drive and inspiration lies with you and you alone.

You have a responsibility to yourself, and those around you, to create a life as high in quality, fun and joy as possible. Putting enough energy and focus into nurturing yourself is a powerful way of helping that life to come about.

Think about this, and consider the techniques I have suggested as you make your stress management action plan below.

Stress management action plan

Having looked at the issue of stress from a number of angles, it's now time to summarise what you intend to do.

My stress management programme will focus on the following strategies:

1 _____

_____

_____

2 _____

_____

_____

3 _____

_____

_____

My stress management programme will focus on the following strategies: (cont.)

4 _____

_____

_____

5 _____

_____

_____

Now relating back to the work that you did earlier on goals, express your commitment as SMART goals!

Summary:
nurture yourself and survive the pressure

1 Some stress is good. It helps us perform at our best.

2 However, we live in a culture where too much emphasis is placed on working hard, and not enough on the long-term consequences. We need to keep work in perspective.

3 First identify the people, circumstances or situations which cause you stress. Then take action to change these for the better.

4 Mellow out. Smell the roses. Take regular breaks and recuperate.

5 Try to be more of a type B. When it rains, let it.

6 Spend more time around people who make you laugh.

7 Look after yourself physically. Eat the right foods, take exercise, get enough sleep.

Principle 8 Believe ...

... in yourself

Whether you think you can, or think you can't, you're usually right!

Henry Ford

Overview

By the end of this chapter you will:

➤ understand the power of self-belief

➤ know how to believe in yourself and your goals

➤ be able to dismiss the negative views of others

➤ create an inspiring, achievable vision of your future.

Your journey so far and the road ahead

If you've read the rest of this book you will have come through a process. Hopefully you are now in a strong position to say:

➤ 'I know what I want.'

➤ 'I know where to focus my energy, time and attention in order to get it.'

➤ 'I know how to organise my day and my schedules to be more effective.'

➤ 'My environment no longer hinders me. In fact it is a wonderful place in which to work and be creative.'

➤ 'I have strategies to maximise the value of my working relationships with my colleagues.'

➤ 'I am motivated and understand the value of action.'

➤ 'I think creatively about the problems that I face.'

All that remains is for you to go off and implement these plans. A piece of cake? Of course not. Change is hard. Even small changes. And the more changes this book has prompted you to commit to, the harder it will be. Ultimately, whether you succeed or not will have nothing to do with this book. All it has done is offer some pointers, apply a bit of common sense and (hopefully) make some helpful suggestions that you find useful. The real power for positive change will come from within you. The final question I have for you is this. Do you really *believe* that you can achieve your most ambitious and precious goals?

The power of belief

There are two types of belief. Empowering belief and disempowering belief. Think of people's attitudes to a glass half filled with water – some see the glass to be half full and others see it as half empty. Does it really matter which type of person you are? If you want to maximise your potential and achieve everything you possibly can – yes it does!

I think it goes without saying that positive, optimistic mindsets built on empowering beliefs about yourself will result in a more rich and fulfilled life than will negative, pessimistic and disempowering mindsets. Consider the following table which demonstrates and summarises some of the thoughts that result from such mental states.

Positive mindset	Negative mindset
I can do this	I'll probably fail
If I fail, at least I'll learn something	When I fail, I'll look ridiculous
Here is an opportunity	This new situation is threatening
We can reach agreement	I must win the argument (whether I'm right or wrong)
People are basically good	People are basically bad
I like to give	I like others to give to me
I am in control	Others are in control

How belief affects performance

Our ability to perform, to excel, is affected directly by which of the two mindsets we choose to adopt. (And I do say 'choose' advisedly because there is a great deal of evidence that we can train ourselves to think positively). It doesn't matter if you are taking part in your first marathon, going for a job interview or whatever, you are almost bound to fail with a negative attitude. It doesn't matter how big or small, trivial or important the endeavour – belief affects performance. If we believe we will fail, we will fail.

And of course the opposite is true. If we firmly believe we will succeed then we vastly increase our chances of success. We may make some mistakes along the way. But strong positive belief will equip us to do something that is crucial to long-term success. It will help us to *persevere*.

Your brain – friend or foe?

Neurologists and psychologists broadly agree on why a positive belief system is so important to success – and why it is almost impossible to succeed without one.

Case study: In 1959 Roger Bannister ran the first sub four-minute mile in history. People had been trying since the beginning of the modern Olympic movement to break records, but the four-minute barrier was seen as an absolute threshhold that no human could cross. Roger Bannister crossed it – but he is not really the point of this story.

The key point is the dozens of other runners who ran a mile in less than four minutes in the *immediately succeeding months* who are of interest to us. Until Bannister broke through, no one believed that it could be done, and their performance reflected this. No matter how brilliant these athletes were, they couldn't imagine success – and therefore they quite literally couldn't achieve it. But when Bannister created history, when they lost their doubt that the barrier could be broken, it was broken over and over again.

Psychologists argue that athletes' repeated failure in the past was born of an intense subconscious desire to act in accordance with their own beliefs. They simply would not allow themselves to succeed, because they didn't believe that it was possible. Once they positively believed, nothing could hold them back!

The brain is key to all of this. Neurologists argue that the longer one holds onto a belief, whether positive or negative, and the more times such beliefs are repeated, the stronger they become. Every time we think a positive or negative thought (called 'self-talk'), such as 'I am/am not attractive', 'I can/cannot speak in public', or 'we can/cannot achieve our targets', a jolt of electricity passes from one neuron to another through junction points on the surface of the brain called synapses. Eventually, if we repeat the belief enough times, a channel is formed along a specific path. This channel will grow deeper and deeper with each repetition of the thought until no other option is possible for the path of the electrical activity triggered by a specific circumstance or event. In the case of Roger Bannister's contemporaries, they'd 'self-talked' themselves out of running a mile in under four minutes so often, that their brains had no choice but to force them to act in accordance with this 'reality'. Their conscious desire was to break the barrier. Their unconscious certainty was that they never would.

This of course is incredibly exciting. Because it means that, simply by repeating positive beliefs, you can 'remodel' the surface architecture of your brain. You can reprogramme yourself to consciously and unconsciously believe in success. With each repetition you can cut a positive, empowering channel deeper and deeper until there is no other option but to act in accordance with this new reality. When that happens, there will be no holding you back.

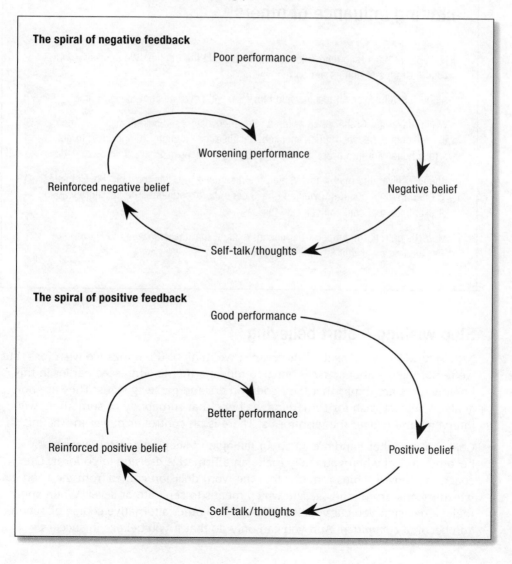

The spiral of negative feedback

Poor performance → Negative belief → Self-talk/thoughts → Reinforced negative belief → Worsening performance

The spiral of positive feedback

Good performance → Positive belief → Self-talk/thoughts → Reinforced positive belief → Better performance

Believe in your goals –
and your ability to achieve them

To make radical changes, to achieve the big goals, you must first believe. You must believe that you are in control and that you have the power to achieve even the most audacious things – that you have the ability to make even your dreams come true. And you must not be put off if others do not share your belief in yourself. Learn to dismiss their negative, limiting influences – how much poorer the world would be if the people described below had not believed in themselves!

Reasons to dismiss the negative, limiting influence of others

In 1962 a Decca recording company executive told the Beatles 'We don't like your sound. Groups of guitars are on the way out'.

Albert Einstein's school teacher told him, 'You will never amount to very much'.

When Alexander Graham Bell asked American investors to back his new invention, the telephone, he was roundly mocked, because they thought it impossible to get a telephone wire into every town in the country – never mind every home.

Spencer Silver, the man who invented the glue used by 3-Ms for their 'Post-It' said 'If I had thought about it, I wouldn't have done the experiment. The literature was full of examples that said you can't do this'.

Mozart's patron, the Emperor Ferdinand, thought that the *Marriage of Figaro* was 'Far too noisy … (with) far too many notes'.

Stop wishing – start believing

Normally when we consider our dreams, we think of the things we wish for – but we're not talking about *wishes* here. To repeat a theme addressed earlier in this book, wishes are things that fairy godmothers and genies give us. They are not goals. When we wish for something we hope that somebody or something will intervene and deliver the wish for us. There is no control or power in wishing.

Goals on the other hand are all about taking and keeping control. A wish becomes a goal when you really make an affirmative *decision* to go for it. Life coach Anthony Robbins remarks that the word decision comes from the Latin *de* which means 'from' and *caedere* which means to separate or sever. When you make a decision you cut yourself off from any other alternative course of action. You become *committed*. And you can only do that if you believe in success.

There is the possibility that you will make a mistake, that the decision will not bring you the rewards that you had hoped, or that you will fail. But it is just a possibility. The following points are certainties:

➤ If, as we've said before, you always do what you've always done, you'll always get what you've always got.

➤ No one discovered a new land without leaving sight of the shore.

➤ You wouldn't have bought this book if you didn't want to change something.

George Bernard Shaw said 'Some men see things as they are and say "why". I dream of things that never were and say "why not"'. So say 'why not?'. List the obstacles. Make plans to overcome them. Believe you can do it.

Create an inspiring vision

Picture the future

You cannot succeed until you feel free to fail, and imagining future success does more than anything else to set you free.

Charles W. McCoy

Unfulfilled potential is a tragedy. Don't let it happen to you! One way of clarifying what a fulfilled future might look like is to create an inspiring vision. Picture a future packed with wonderful outcomes. These could focus on:

➤ personal life, home and family

➤ career and work

➤ health and well-being

➤ finances

➤ relationships

➤ community

➤ intellectual life

➤ spirituality

➤ anything else that's important to you

➤ any combination of the above.

Make sure that the vision fits

Make sure these outcomes fit well with your roles and values. Don't dream about over-landing to Bhutan if you've got a child just about to start school and you want to be around for them. Whatever you put into your vision make it as detailed as possible. Paint a picture of this future life and make it as convincing as possible. Such a vision will help you keep day-to-day challenges in perspective and help you deal with small setbacks or defeats. It will help you be patient, build slowly, keep focused and work little by little towards your future reality.

Letters from the future and providence maps

A technique which has been widely used to confirm the picture is to send yourself a 'letter from the future'. To do this:

> Choose a date months, or even years ahead (depending on how long you reasonably expect it might take to achieve the outcomes that make up your vision).

> Imagine that you have achieved everything that you set out to do. Everything has gone better than you could have expected and things have turned out just as you wanted.

> Now write yourself a letter telling yourself about it all. Say what you've done, how it makes you feel. Demonstrate how this future you is living a life more in tune with their values and roles than you are today. What improvements have been made? What benefits have accrued? What negative or unhelpful behaviours or circumstances have you left behind?

> Keep the letter in your diary, or wherever you have recorded your goals, and review it regularly with your goals. Read it when you need inspiration and when you'd like to measure how far you've come as you generate the outcomes that make up the vision.

An alternative method is to create a 'providence map'. Some people find that they can make their dreams and aspirations more tangible by using pictures and images to create a visual representation of what the future holds. To make one of these, you'll need a flip-chart-sized piece of card, scissors, glue, magazines and coloured pens. Now go through the magazines to find images that reflect what you would like in your life. These may be material things, such as a house with a garden, or a top of the range car, or they may be pictures of exotic locations to represent travel, or hobbies you'd like to take up. Alternatively they may focus on helping others, career changes or skills you'd like to acquire. Cut them out and arrange them on the board. Whenever you come across an appropriate image, add it to the board. Try and spot themes and trends. Write notes to yourself or inspirational quotes directly onto the emerging picture. Let the developing illustration confirm your desires and motivate you to make concrete plans to achieve them.

When you are happy that the map is complete, try and express it as SMART goals, as we discussed in chapter 1. The process should be the same, but the goals should be bigger, more ambitious and extraordinarily exciting. At this point you will have come full circle. If you need to re-read the book to reinforce the messages and techniques, go ahead. Success is a habit.

They say that there is no such thing as good luck, there is only a place in the future where preparation meets opportunity. With that in mind, I've only got one more thing to say to you ... GOOD LUCK!

Your personal effectiveness master plan

If you've reached this point in the book you've done a lot of thinking and planning. Now you can pull it all together into a single master plan. A key benefit of doing this will be to reinforce the decisions you have made. You will also have all your conclusions and decisions in one place, making it easier for you to check these stated intentions against your actual behaviour over the coming months.

This guide shows you how to produce your personal master plan. It highlights the key points and charts to complete. Follow these signposts to write up your own plan. If you need help along the way, the page references show you where in the book you can find more information.

Creating a personal vision

Roles and values

(see pages 10–20)

Make two lists – one identifying your main roles (remember to prioritise them) and one listing your key values.

Set goals

Your goal programme

(see pages 29–30)

List your roles, and against each one, note down the related goals you wish to achieve.

Golden goals

(see pages 30–31)

Remember the golden goal method – take your top ten most important goals from the list you've generated above and summarise them. These are your golden goals – those that are most important and would make the biggest difference to you. Then rank these golden goals into order of preference.

Focus on activities which make a real difference

Bubble delegation

(see pages 36–41)

Blow some delegation bubbles. Draw a chart with three columns – use the headings given below. See pages 38–39 to remind yourself about the golden rules for successful delegation.

Task	To whom could I delegate it?	Which golden rules do I have to apply and how?

Structural delegation

(see pages 41–45)

1   Establish your fundamental outcome statement (in other words, what are you for?). Complete this sentence: 'The outcomes attached to my post which must be achieved are …'

2   Make a list of your critical priority tasks (i.e. those tasks which will help you achieve these outcomes).

3   Identify people you need to inform/negotiate with to ensure you can focus more of your attention on these tasks.

4   Name the tasks you can permanently reassign to others. (These tasks should match other people's FORs more closely than your own.)

Urgency versus importance

(see pages 45–51)

Go back to your urgent versus important matrix and prioritise some wasteful activities to lose. Then decide on a better way to spend the time you will save. Use the following headings in your list to help you:

Futile or wasteful activity to lose	Time saved per week	New achievement activity to substitute

Structure your day

Planner

(see pages 55–57)

Do you have a suitable planner? If not what sort do you prefer? When will you acquire one?

Prioritising your to-do list

(see pages 58–61)

What lower priority tasks can you negotiate away? Make a list, using the headings below, to help you achieve this.

Task   **Person to negotiate with**   **Action by (give yourself a deadline)**

Remember the one-stage planning rules

Use the popcorn technique

(see pages 62–63)

The popcorn technique recognises that your day will be filled, even if you only programme in enough activity to fill half of it. This means you have to get rid of some of your tasks. What action do you need to take? What negotiation do you need to make? Who do you need to liaise with, if you are to use the popcorn technique successfully?

Plan continually

(see pages 63–64)

What action do you need to take to remind yourself to plan continually?

Multi-achieve

(see pages 64–65)

What multi-achieving activities can you put into your programme? Remember my example. If you want to get fit and spend more time with the kids, take them swimming or go for a walk.

Find your high energy window

(see pages 65–66)

Ask yourself the following questions:

> When is your high energy window likely to be each day?

> What actions do you need to take, or which people do you need to speak to to restructure your schedule to provide space in your diary at this time?

> Once you have freed up time, what key activities will you accomplish in your window?

> Where will your sanctuary be? If you haven't got one, what actions do you need to take to make a sanctuary?

Use the hidden hour

(see pages 66–68)

1   Make a list of typical pockets of time when your brain isn't working. Such as waiting for your PC to boot up in the morning or when you are ready to begin a meeting in your office a few minutes before everyone else arrives.

2   Make a list of the kind of 'no-brainer' activities which you intend to slot into these pockets. Remember that they should be do-able in 5–10 minutes, have no deadlines, require no referral to others, require no follow up and require no energy.

3   Break up large tasks into smaller ones: use the sliced loaf technique. Choose a large task and break it down into smaller constituent parts. Then schedule these into your planner.

Protect yourself from the time stealers

Saying 'no'

(see pages 71–73)

Produce a 'Just Say No' action plan – write down a list of people who you need to say 'no' to and note down your strategy.

Managing meetings

(see pages 74–80)

Begin by asking 'why do we need this meeting?' Then ask 'will the outcomes be worth it?'

1   Begin by asking 'why do we need this meeting?' Then ask 'will the outcomes be worth it?' Name some less than purposeful meetings that you can dispense with.

2   Suggest how you can improve your own behaviour to make the meetings you attend more successful.

3   Which of the following meeting rules can you introduce your team/colleagues to? Do you need to work on a meetings improvement strategy?

   a) clarify objectives

   b) have a timed agenda

   c) summarise regularly

   d) agree action points

   e) think about the environment.

Dealing with interruptions

(see pages 81–84)

Record the specific techniques you think would reduce the number and length of the interruptions you suffer from. Think about who the main offenders are; can you reprogramme their behaviour? Identify whether there are periods of the day when you are likely to get more interruptions than otherwise. Can you create a schedule to accommodate these?

Organise your environment to maximise efficiency

Creating a more organised working environment
(see pages 88–92)

1   Think of strategies you can use to achieve a more organised working environment. How will you:

   a) Attract less paper?

   b) Have one project on your desk at any one time?

   c) Deal with each piece of paper immediately?

2   Make a list of the paper products which:

   a) You can act on immediately

   b) You can usually file for later

   c) You can give it to someone else

   d) You can immediately throw away.

Ergonomic improvements
(see pages 92–93)

What ergonomic improvements can you make to your working environment? What actions do you need to take (research/approvals/budget commitments etc.)? Please remember that you must seek proper advice from a qualified person, such as your doctor or a qualified physiotherapist, before taking any action that might have repercussions on your health.

Can you work from home?
(see pages 94–95)

What actions do you need to take to create an effective and comfortable home office?

Switching off your mobile
(see page 95)

1   Name the worst thing that could happen if you left your mobile switched off.

2   Now list the potential benefits.

3   When could you switch off your mobile (e.g. when travelling on trains, over lunch, during your high energy window) when you'd benefit more than you'd lose?

Managing e-mails
(see pages 96–97)

What actions do you plan to take to manage your e-mails better?

Nurture yourself

1 What actions can you take to eliminate key stress agents?
(see pages 110–113)

2 What strategies will you use to manage your stress?
(see pages 113–118)

Further reading

Goal setting and personal achievement

Rouillard, Larrie	*Goals and Goal Setting* (Kogan Page)
Covey, Stephen	*First Things First* (Simon & Schuster)
Covey, Stephen	*The 7 Habits of Highly Effective People* (Simon & Schuster)
Ghazi, Polly & Jones, Judy	*The Downshifter's Guide to Happier and Simpler Living* (Hodder & Stoughton)
Koch, Richard	*The 80/20 Principle* (Nicholas Brealey)
Tracy, Brian	*Thinking Big* (Simon & Schuster)
Downing Orr, Kristina	*Get the Life You Want* (Thorsons)
Harrold, Fiona	*Be Your Own Life Coach* (Hodder & Stoughton)
Qubein, Nido	*Stairway to Success* (John Wiley and Sons)
McGraw, Dr Phillip	*Life Strategies* (Vermillion)
Johnson, Dr Spencer	*Who Moved My Cheese?* (Vermillion)
Gaskell, Carole	*Transform Your Life* (Thorsons)
Robbins, Anthony	*Awaken the Giant Within* (Simon & Schuster)
Turner, Colin	*The Eureka Principle* (Element)
Parsons, Rob	*The Heart of Success* (Hodder & Stoughton)

Time management and personal effectiveness

Lakein, Alan	*How to Get Control of Your Time and Your Life* (Gower)
Noon, James	*A Time* (Van Nostrand Reinhold)
Forster, Mark	*Get Everything Done and Still Have Time to Play* (Hodder & Stoughton)

Treacy, Declan	*Clear Your Desk* (Century Business)
Adair, John & Allen, Melanie	*Time Management and Personal Development* (Hawksmere)
Maitland, Iain	*Managing Your Time* (CIPD)
Young, Stephen	*How to Manage Time and Set Priorities* (Random House)

Stress management

Carnegie, Dale	*How to stop Worrying and Start Living* (Mandarin)
Skinner, Robin & Cleese, John	*Life and How to Survive It* (Methuen)
Harrison, Eric	*Teach Yourself to Meditate* (Piatkus)
Chaitow, Eric	*The Stress Protection Plan* (Thorsons)
Atkinson, Jacqueline	*Coping With Stress at Work* (Thorsons)
Wilkinson, Professor Greg	*The BMA Family Doctor Guide to Stress* (Dorling Kindersley)

About DSC

The Directory of Social Change (DSC) aims to help voluntary and community organisations become more effective. A charity ourselves, we are the leading provider of information and training for the voluntary sector.

We run more than 350 training courses each year as well as conferences, many of which run on an annual basis. We also publish an extensive range of guides, handbooks and CD-ROMs for the voluntary sector, covering subjects such as fundraising, management, communication, finance and law. Our trusts database is available on both a CD-ROM and a subscription website.

Charityfair, the annual three-day conference, events programme and exhibition, is organised by DSC and takes place each spring.

For details of all our activities, and to order publications and book courses, go to www.dsc.org.uk or call 020 7391 4800.

Selected DSC books and courses

Books

Developing your Organisation, Alan Lawrie

The Complete Guide to Creating and Managing New Projects, 2nd edition, Alan Lawrie

A Management Companion for Voluntary Organisations, Tim Cook and Guy Braithwaite

Managing without profit, Mike Hudson

Courses

Marketing for the Small Organisation, Mark Butcher and Sahara Consultancy

Writing Effective Promotional Material, Chris Wells and Mark Butcher

Time Management, Ailsa Masterson, Candy Smith and Richard Peters

Performing under Pressure, Gill Tree

Taking Control of Your Stress, Christine Thornton

Assertiveness – Mixed, Joan Browne and Barwen Training